Pembroke Castle

THE CASTLES OF

SOUTH-WEST WALES

Mike Salter

FOLLY PUBLICATIONS

ACKNOWLEDGEMENTS

The illustrations in this book are mostly the product of the author's own site surveys from the 1977 to 1996 and the old postcards reproduced are from his collection. Most of the plans of large stone buildings are on a scale of 1:800 but some smaller buildings are shown at 1:400. Other plans are at 1:1250 and earthworks are mostly at 1:2000.

Thanks are due to Max Barfield of Hyde in Cheshire for providing word processor facilities, the loan of a camera, and help with transport. She also checked the text. Phil Hellin of Welshpool took the photo of Laugharne on page 34. Thanks are also due to various people who allowed the author access to sites in their care.

AUTHOR'S NOTES

This series of books (see a full list inside the back cover) are intended as portable field guides giving as much information and illustrative material as possible in volumes of modest size, weight and price. Quite a lot of information is given on lesser known buildings not adequately described and illustrated elsewhere. The aim has been to mention, where the information is known to the author, owners or custodians of castles who erected or altered parts of the buildings, and those who were the first or last of a line to hold an estate or be honoured with an office or title. Those in occupation of the buildings at the time of historic events such as sieges are also sometimes named. Other owners and occupants whose lives had little effect on the buildings are not often mentioned, nor are ghost stories, myths and legends.

The books are intended to be used in conjunction with the Ordnance Survey 1;50,000 scale maps. Grid references are given in the gazetteers together with a coding system indicating which buildings can be visited or easily seen by the public which is explained on page 11. Many of the earthworks which are briefly described on pages 46-47 and 86-87 lie on private lands some distance from public roads and paths. Some are hidden by trees and scrub so visiting them can be difficult and in most cases is not recommended except by those making a special study.

It was thought convenient to divide the descriptions of the stone castles into two gazetteers, one dealing with the former counties of Cardigan (now called Ceredigion) and Carmarthen, and the other with Pembrokeshire. Deciding what spellings to use for some place names and personal names has not been easy and the author apologises to anyone who is upset by his use of a particular spelling. There have been many changes to spellings of Welsh place names during the 20th century, particularly in the last few years, and consequently there is little agreement between spellings used on the various editions of the O.S. maps and in the various reference books, some of which were published much earlier this century. On the whole English place names and spellings have been used except where Welsh names (such as Llansteffan or Ceredigion) have been reinstated for almost universal usage. Readers should also be aware that many of the earthworks are known by different writers under different names. Some earthworks have their own names; others are listed under that of the nearest village, church, farm or other reference point.

Each level of a building is called a storey in this book, the basement being the first storey and more or less at courtyard level unless specifically mentioned as otherwise.

All measurements quoted in the text and the scales on the plans are metric because the author measured the buildings in metres. For those who feel the need to make a conversion 3 metres is almost 10 feet. Unless specifically stated as otherwise all dimensions are external at or near ground level but above the plinth if there is one.

Old photograph of north tower of middle ward, Aberystwyth.

CONTENTS

Maps and notes on other sites occur at the ends of the gazetteers.

INTRODUCTION

The parts of Wales which from the mid 13th century until 1974 were called by English speakers the counties of Cardigan, Carmarthen and Pembroke, and more recently collectively known as Dyfed, were not invaded by the Normans then occupying England until after 1093. In that year the native ruler of Deheubarth, Rhys ap Tewdwr, was killed fighting the Normans near Brecon and the invaders took advantage of the usual Welsh inheritance problem of squabbles amongst his successors. Roger de Montgomery, Earl of Shrewsbury, pushed as far as west Pembroke and Cardigan, where he established defensible lordly residences of a type known to the Normans as castles. Such buildings were previously unknown in this part of Wales. Earl Roger and his followers occupied much of the coastal lands but the Welsh counter-attacked in 1094 and drove the Normans out except from Pembroke itself. The Montgomery family were defeated and exiled for rebellion against Henry I of England in 1102 and their place in South-West Wales was taken by the de Clare family, named after their seat of Clare in Suffolk. Gilbert de Clare was created Earl of Pembroke in 1138 by King Stephen. By this time Norman and Flemish lords were securely in possession of the southern half of what became Pembrokeshire, plus the coasts around Cardigan and Carmarthen, the castles of which two places were to later become royal centres of administration and justice. The Normans divided the land into manors which were mostly held by knights in return for military service to baronial overlords. The knights in turn built castles, usually of more modest size and strength than those maintained by the barons and the English Crown.

The building of castles of mortared stone required many years of peace and the services of masons not readily available in the late 11th and early 12th centuries. Instead the castles of this period were quickly and cheaply constructed of earth and wood by gangs of slave labourers aided and directed by fighting men. Early castles tended to take two forms, mottes and ringworks. A motte was a mound created either by piling up earth from a surrounding ditch or by cutting through the neck of a spur or promontory. On the summit would stand a timber tower containing living rooms for the lord and surrounded by a small palisaded court. The mottes in South-West Wales appear to all be of the period 1110-45. The earliest castles at Pembroke and Cardigan were ringworks and this type remained in fashion until the early 13th century. They have high ramparts enclosing courts usually between 20m and 35m across, natural features being used where possible and sections of rampart and ditch being dispensed with where steep natural slopes made them unnecessary. Ringworks are bigger than most motte summits, but smaller than the enclosures called baileys which often accompany mottes and ringworks. Baileys can be up to 90m across, although 45-60m would be more normal, and were defended by a palisaded rampart with a ditch in front. Ringworks and baileys contained an array of wooden buildings comprising a hall, chapel, the lord's room or solar, workshops, stables, a granary, and other typical farm buildings. Mottes with summits less than 15m across without baileys would have only afforded limited accommodation and were probably only occupied for a few years.

The ringwork at Old Aberystwyth

Ringwork at Llanrhystud

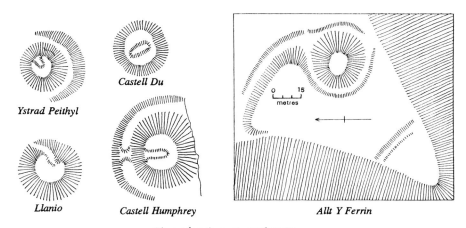

Ystrad Peithyl

Castell Du

Llanio

Castell Humphrey

Allt Y Ferrin

Plans of early castle earthworks

There was much military activity in Ceredigion (Cardiganshire) and Carmarthen in the 1130s, 40s and 50s with castles being erected, captured and burnt as the Welsh squabbled both with the Normans and among themselves, whilst the de Clares waged a new campaign in 1158. Then things quietened down until the 1190s as an able new Welsh ruler of the now rather truncated Deheubarth arose in Rhys ap Gruffydd, better known as The Lord Rhys. Wood and earth remained the normal materials for castle building in this area until the end of the century, but it is possible that parts of the existing walls at Rhys' chief seat at Dinefwr were built by him, and he is said to have built a stone castle at Aberteifi (Cardigan). Cilgerran, a very rocky site unsuited for earthworks and palisades, seems to have had modest and primitive stone buildings from the early 12th century. Manorbier has a hall block probably of the 1160s capable of independent defence. Over unlighted cellars it contained a hall with a buttery at one end with a dark solar above the buttery. Some of the walling at Carmarthen could be of the 1180s. Haverfordwest has two somewhat altered walls remaining of a rectangular tower keep of about the same period containing a hall over a basement, probably with a private room or solar for the lord above, whilst Carew has part of an early gatehouse. Probably of the 1190s are the walled courts on the motte and ringwork at Wiston and Llansteffan respectively. In each case the wall was only about 3 to 4m high above the inside, but rather higher on the outside. The structure at Wiston is of a type now referred to as a shell keep. The wall at Llansteffan enclosed a much larger area and was probably too thin to carry a wall-walk as well as a parapet.

Pembroke Castle

Of great importance are the developments at Pembroke in the 1190s, when the castle was rebuilt by William Marshal after he married a de Clare heiress and became earl. A roughly triangular bailey was created by building a breastwork on the two well protected sites and a high curtain wall on the other side. This wall was flanked by a square turret, a small round tower, and a large U-shaped projection containing the gateway. Immediately behind the wall stands a huge round tower which would have then been known as a donjon, although the word keep is normally used now. Some of the 12th century keeps in England contain fine halls, bedchambers and chapels but the Pembroke keep was mainly a military post dominating the defences, providing a secure place for valuables and prisoners, and acting as a final refuge if the bailey defences were penetrated. The rooms inside it were dark and poorly provided with amenities, and in any case a hall and other domestic buildings were erected in stone to one side of it at about the same time. In the early 13th century the castle was greatly strengthened and enlarged to become one of the finest British castles when an outer bailey was added with a high wall flanked at close intervals by round towers and entered through a gatehouse with complex planning.

The new works at Pembroke inspired the building of many other stone castles with round flanking towers and round keeps in South-West Wales during the 13th century. There are a number of surviving records of additions, alterations and repairs to buildings in the 14th and 15th centuries but no records of the construction of any of the many 13th century castles in South-West Wales remain except that begun in 1277 by Edward I at Aberystwyth. Consequently dating the castles more accurately is a matter of guesswork and analogy with other buildings. Of English-built castles of the period between the death of the first William Marshal in 1219 and the campaign by Llywelyn ap Gruffudd of North Wales in 1257, during which many Norman castles in South-west Wales were captured and burnt, are a walled court with round corner towers at Manorbier, two substantial round towers and the walls and gates of two courts at Cilgerran, minimal remains of round tower keeps at Llawhaden, Llansteffan, Narberth, a square gatehouse at Llansteffan, walling and perhaps a tower at Cardigan, and probably the shell keep at Carmarthen. Welsh-built castles of the same period include massive round keeps with small courts at Dinefwr and Dryslwyn, footings of a rectangular keep at Ystrad Meurig, and possibly some walling at Carreg Cennan. The small courts with pairs of towers at Benton and Laugharne may be of this period or slightly later. The unusual U-shaped keep at Roch and the chapel block and outer court at Manorbier are both thought to be of the 1260s.

In the 1270s Edward I defeated Llywelyn ap Gruffydd and hemmed him into Snowdonia by building several new castles, including that at Aberystwyth. Llywelyn was killed in a skirmish near Builth in 1282, and although there were later Welsh uprisings they were of short duration and were contained by the chain of new castles. Not until the rising of Owain Glyndwr in the first decade of the 15th century did the Welsh again seriously challenge the might of the English Crown. Aberystwyth is a concentric castle inspired by that of Caerphilly begun by Gilbert de Clare, Earl of Gloucester in 1268. Excavations have shown that the original design was not fully concentric, but as completed in the 1280s the castle had a lozenge shaped inner ward closely surrounded by an outer ward of the same shape. Both lines of defence had round corner towers and each had a twin-towered gatehouse, the inner gatehouse being a huge self contained structure containing quarters for the garrison commander on the now destroyed upper storeys. Laugharne has an outer ward of the same shape and date of that at Aberystwyth, also with a twin-towered gatehouse on an obtuse angle in the middle of the landward side. There the inner ward, (probably a generation or two older), lies on the far side, not in the middle. Also assumed to be of the period 1275-90 are the square inner ward with boldly projecting round corner towers at Kidwelly (which has several parallels in Ireland), a similar layout but with a longer and more irregularly shaped court at Narberth, courts with D-shaped towers and a twin-towered gatehouses at Llansteffan and Newport, a court with two ranges of apartments, a round tower and a gatehouse (now destroyed) at Haverfordwest, a hall block with rectangular wings at Llawhaden, a D-shaped tower and a small court on the motte at Llandovery, and the east range with a polygonal chapel tower and one U-shaped tower at Carew.

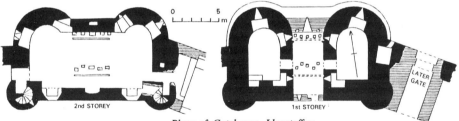

0   5
⊢⊢⊢⊢⊢⊢ m

2nd STOREY

1st STOREY

LATER GATE

Plans of Gatehouse, Llansteffan

Llansteffan Castle

Old print of Carmarthen Castle

The west range containing the main hall at Carew was added in a separate campaign c1290-1320. It has two boldly projecting corner towers rising from square bases with tall pyramidal spurs or beaks. Round or polygonal towers with spurs are a characteristic feature of military works of the period 1275-1310 in South Wales. In the area we are concerned with here, spurs also occur on D-shaped towers at Cardigan, Carmarthen and Newport, and on a twin towered gatehouse and one of two corner towers on the innermost of two square courts at Carreg Cennan. Contemporary with the hall block at Carew are the domestic range and the adjoining chapel tower plus the semi-circular outer court with three towers (originally open-backed) and two gatehouses at Kidwelly, the curtain walls with polygonal towers and two ranges of apartments at Llawhaden, a hall block originally flanked by five D-shaped towers and a twin-towered gatehouse at Picton, the inner gatehouse at Manorbier, a gateway with round towers at Upton, and at least one of the domestic ranges and perhaps the outer ward defences at Dryslwyn. The remains at Tenby and the embattled hall-houses of Eastington and Newhouse could be of any time during the late 13th century or early 14th century, as could the modest block with at least one round turret at Roche.

Newcastle Emlyn

At Dinefwr new domestic buildings were added some time between the 1320s and 1400, and the Bonville family built a now-vanished tower near Saundersfoot, but many of the castles were neglected for fifty years after the Edwardian wave of building subsided in the 1320s. Both England and Wales were peaceful after 1330 when Edward III began to govern for himself and the castles were often left without proper garrisons. In Pembrokeshire the castles of Cilgerran, Manorbier, Pembroke and Tenby passed by marriage to families which had several other comfortable seats in England. The castles and their lands were simply treated as sources of revenue and were never inhabited by the great lords who owned them. The same fate befell several castles in Carmarthenshire which became part of the Duchy of Lancaster which merged with the Crown on the accession of Henry IV in 1399. Although the thick main walls of castles usually remained sound, parapets soon began to crumble, whilst drawbridges, timber outbuildings, and roofs without proper lead coverings soon began to rot. When Edward III feared a French invasion in the 1370s many castles had to be hastily garrisoned and repaired. Much work was then done at Cilgerran, where a large new tower (now mostly fallen down the cliff) was erected. Of c1380-1400 are the twin-towered outer part of the gatehouse at Llawhaden and the fortified manor house of Angle with two small square towers set at diagonally opposite corners of a moated enclosure. The castles were again pressed into service against Owain Glyndwr in 1403-9, several being captured and others damaged. Considerable rebuilding was done to the gatehouses at Kidwelly and Carmarthen afterwards. In c1455 a gunport was inserted into a tower at Carreg Cennan, a rare instance of such a feature in Wales although gunports of the keyhole type also occur in a square tower of about the same period on the town walls of Tenby. Firearms, gunpowder and cannon are first mentioned in this area much earlier since they appear on a list of munitions at Haverfordwest Castle in 1388. However when Carreg Cennan was dismantled in 1464 to prevent Lancastrian rebels using it as a base for raids, it was not blown up as was the norm in the Civil War two centuries later, but the tops of the walls and towers were thrown down by a large labour force with using picks and bars.

Carmarthen Castle

Tower House at Angle

Inside the court at Carew Castle

Old print of Cardigan Castle

Castles in South-West Wales are mostly built of slabs of limestone in rough courses or uncoursed rubble, with dressed (cut) stones used only for corners and openings. Ashlar was rarely used in this area in the 13th century. Walls were normally whitewashed both inside and out so the buildings would have looked very different from the way they do today. Domestic rooms would have been decorated with murals of biblical or historical scenes predominantly painted in red, yellow and black. Although used in churches, glass was uncommon in secular buildings before the 15th century and up until the 16th century windows were closed with shutters, so that the rooms were dark when the weather was cold or wet. Living rooms usually have fireplaces although some halls were heated by fires in central hearths with a louvre in the roof. Furnishings were sparse in the 13th and 14th centuries, although window embrasures often have built-in stone seats. Great lords circulated from one castle or manor house to another, consuming local agricultural produce on the spot and administering their manorial courts. Servants travelled with them and so did transportable furnishings such as rugs and cooking vessels which were kept in wooden chests. When the lord moved on only a caretaker would be left except when troubled times necessitated the expense of mustering and equipping a permanent garrison. Initially there was little privacy except for the lord and his leading officers. The sharing of beds and communal sleeping in the hall and places of work like the stables or kitchen was common.

In the second half of the 15th century the outer gatehouse at Llansteffan was converted into a self contained residence, the old passageway being blocked and a new gateway of lesser strength being built alongside it. From the 1490s onwards Carew was modernised by Sir Rhys ap Thomas, one of the leading Welshmen of his day, having supported Henry VII at Bosworth. He inserting many mullioned windows into the east and west ranges and their flanking towers. Also a porch was added in front of the hall, and the outer gatehouse was rebuilt. Sir Rhys later added a gallery at Narberth and also modernised Newcastle Emlyn where parts (if not all) of the gatehouse appear to be his work. Of about the same period are a hall, a bakehouse, and another large block in the outer ward at Kidwelly. Llawhaden was kept in repair by the bishops of St Davids until the 1530s, when it was dismantled for its materials by an absentee bishop. Sir John Perrot improved the castles of Laugharne and Carew in the 1580s, adding new ranges in such a way as to greatly increase the accommodation without significantly reducing the strength of the outer defences. The range at Carew contained a long gallery and is particularly impressive, with large regularly spaced mullion-and-transom windows in the upper parts of the walls.

The castles of Aberystwyth, Carew, Carmarthen, Haverfordwest, Laugharne, Newcastle Emlyn, Pembroke, Picton, Roch and the walled town of Tenby all suffered sieges during the Civil Wars of the 1640s, several of them changing hands more than once. Picton and Upton are still inhabited and have consequently seen considerable alterations and extensions in the last two hundred years, whilst Amroth has been rebuilt out of existence, and Dale very nearly so. The other castles named above were all wrecked either during sieges or by dismantling afterwards to save the victorious Parliamentarians the cost and effort of garrisoning them. Carew has remains of a ravelin in front of the outer gate whilst at Pembroke in the walls of the inner ward were dismantled to provide material for thickening the outer wall against cannon. Of the period after the Civil War is the round summer house, originally with a conical roof, built on the stump of the keep at Dinefwr a century after the castle had been left to become a scenic ruin visible from a new mansion. In the 19th century ruins at places which were beginning to draw visitors, such as Aberystwyth, began to be made safe, whilst the gatehouse at Newport was converted into house and Roch was restored. In the 1930s Benton was again made habitable and at Pembroke the outer parts of the towers blown up in 1648 were restored. Much conservation has taken place in the last fifty years. Excavations have revealed buried footings of the inner wards and their buildings at Aberystwyth and Dryslwyn and the keep at Wiston has just been cleared.

PUBLIC ACCESS TO THE CASTLES

C   Ruins maintained by Cadw (fee payable at some sites).
F   Ruins normally freely accessible to the public at any time.
G   Grounds or gardens only are open to the public (fee usually payable).
O   Opened to the public by private owners or trusts or local councils.
V   Not open but visible at close range from public open space, path, or road.

Laugharne Castle

CASTLES OF CARMARTHENSHIRE AND CEREDIGION

ABERYSTWYTH SN 579816 & 585790

The earliest castle in this district was the ringwork and bailey strongly sited on a hill 2km south of the present town. The ringwork measures 40m by 30m and rises 5m above a D-shaped bailey to the SW measuring about 40m by 37m. This castle was built in 1110 by Gilbert de Clare and resisted a Welsh attack in 1116, but in 1136 it was captured and burnt. It must have been restored soon afterwards, for in 1142 it was burnt again during fighting amongst the Welsh themselves. The de Clares recovered their territories here in 1158 but lost them again in 1164 when Rhys ap Gruffydd burnt the castle of "Aberheidol", which may either refer to a long lost earthwork at Plas Crug in the Rheidol valley or to the older site which Gerald of Wales refers to as in use in 1188. The castle at Aberystwyth destroyed by Maelgwn ap Rhys in 1208 in order to prevent Llywelyn ab Iorwerth from using it may have been at Plas Crug (SN 590812) but the remains of a rectangular court and square tower there removed in the 1960s may have only been an 18th century folly. Llywelyn restored the castle (wherever it was) and held it until he was defeated by King John in 1211. A new castle was then built by Faulkes de Breaute which was immediately burnt by the Welsh. It was quickly restored but was captured in 1221 by Llywelyn ab Iorwerth.

Postern Tower, Aberystwyth

Aberystwyth Castle

Following Edward I's campaign against Llywelyn ap Gruffydd in 1277 work was begun in August of that year on constructing the present castle now known as Aberystwyth, although this name only came into general use in the 15th century, early records calling the castle and borough Lampadarn (after Llanbadarn Fawr, which lies 2km to the east). In October 1279 those working on the castle and town defences included 176 masons, 14 carpenters, 5 smiths, 2 plumbers and 1,120 labourers. In 1282 the constable, Bogo de Knoville, was treacherously captured by the Welsh at Llanbadarn after accepting an invitation to dine with the local Welsh ruler Gruffydd ap Maredudd, whose men then captured the unfinished castle in a surprise attack. It was said to have been destroyed but the damage cannot have been great as deliveries of lead in 1283 suggest that some of the buildings were ready for roofing. The King stayed at the castle in November 1284, by which time it must have been substantially complete, but further works were ordered, and in 1286 an account mentions work on the King's Chamber, a block on the west side containing a stable and bakehouse, and a barbican towards the town. In 1287 the castle, newly furnished with timber fighting galleries by the carpenters Robert and Nicholas, successfully resisted a rebellion by Rhys ap Maredudd. Further repairs and improvements followed, until by 1289 £4,300 had been spent on the works. In 1294 the Welsh again rose in revolt and besieged the castle for several months after murdering its custodian, Geoffrey Clement. Supplies brought in by sea enabled the garrison to hold out until the revolt collapsed.

Inner gatehouse at Aberystwyth

The castle needed repairs to tower roofs and the outer drawbridge by 1321 and by 1343, when the Black Prince took possession, the list of depredations included rotting drawbridges, the ruination of the defences of the outer ward on the west side by the sea, and decay in the main gatehouse, the Long Chamber, the King's Hall, the Old Hall, the kitchen, the bakehouse and stable, and the old and new granaries. Just £6 was spent on repairs, although the survey estimated the work would cost £306, but the drawbridges were rebuilt shortly afterwards. Gradually, as conditions became more secure, the garrison was reduced. John de Scudamore had 50 crossbowmen and archers under him in 1298, whilst Roger de Coteford, constable in 1347, had only 20 men, and by 1371 just 10 longbowmen were stationed in the castle.

In 1401 Owain Glyndwr's forces burnt the town but failed to take the castle. It finally fell to the Welsh in 1404 after being blockaded for many months when its supply ship, La Laurence of Bristol, was captured by Henry Dwnn and William Gwyn. In 1406 Prince Henry (later Henry V) besieged a Welsh garrison under Rhys Ddu in the castle. Both cannon (an early record of their use) and conventional siege engines were used against the defences, but the Welsh held out, and Glyndwr only lost the use of the castle in 1408 when Prince Henry laid a more successful siege against it. Four French prisoners captured in 1415 at Agincourt were housed in the castle, and in 1428 monks of Strata Florida Abbey were incarcerated in it after a scandalous raid upon their monastery by a large force led by John ap Rhys, Abbot of Aberconwy.

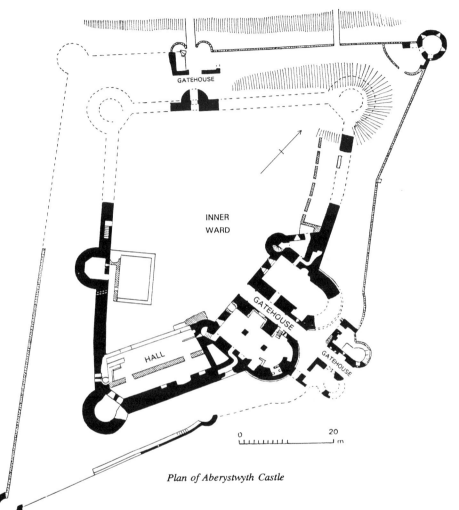

Plan of Aberystwyth Castle

In 1637 Charles I allowed Thomas Bushell to set up a mint in the decayed castle, silver and lead being supplied by local mines. The mint was transferred elsewhere when war broke out in 1642, but the castle remained a bullion store. From his profits Bushell raised and equipped a regiment for the King from the local miners. In 1644 the Royalist garrison sallied to attack a Parliamentary force at Llanbadarn but was repulsed, 13 of them being drowned in the mill pond as they fled back to the castle. A siege mounted in 1645 dragged on until the following year, when Colonel Whitely surrendered the place to Colonel Rice Powell. In 1647 John Port, a London lead factor, managed to steal coins and bullion worth £30,000 from the castle, plus 500 tons of lead left awaiting shipment at Aberdovey. In September 1649 Lieutenant Colonel Dawking and Captain Barbour supervised the blowing up of the castle defences. Locals soon began to take stone from the ruins although fines for unauthorised removal were imposed in 1739. Some repairs were executed in 1835, and some clearance of the gateway carried out in 1844, as by then tourists were beginning to flock to the town.

The castle lies on the west end of a low rocky promontory formed by the sea to the west and north and the Rheidol estuary to the south. The inner ward was roughly rectangular, with a round tower 8m in diameter at the more or less right-angled west corner, elongated D-shaped towers at the more acute north and south corners, and a huge twin towered gatehouse occupying the flattened east corner. The curtains were up to 2.4m thick and enclosed a court 54m long by 45m wide. At a distance varying from 10m to 15m lay an outer wall enclosing the middle ward. It also had round towers at the west, north and south corners, and a twin-towered gateway on the east, beyond which was a barbican. The NE and SE sides of the middle ward are each bowed inwards, having two straight walls meeting at an angle marked by a turret. A triangular outer ward with sides about 60m long now lacking any defences (a section of ditch on the NE was filled in when the Promenade was built in 1901) lay to seaward on the NW and was reached by gateways through both the inner and outer ward curtains, the outer gate being twin towered, whilst the inner gate was a single D-shaped tower pierced by a passageway. This inner NW gateway is now the only part of the inner ward to stand complete with its parapet. Except for sections which adjoined the missing west tower, and a short section south of the east gate, the wall of the middle ward still forms a circuit. It forms a retaining wall 6m high above the rock-cut outer ditch but has no more than a 19th century parapet above the ground level inside, and the NW gateway is in the same state. The north and south towers of the middle ward stand somewhat higher, but the east gateway is more fragmentary.

Until recent excavation all that remained visible of the inner ward apart from the NW gatehouse was a high fragment of the round outer part of the southern gatehouse, and the lower parts of the rest of the building, which was 27m wide. Each tower 18.5m long contained just one large U-shaped chamber with a pair of loops at the west end, a loop commanding the outer part of the entrance passage, and a doorway leading on to the central part of the passage, which had a portcullis and two leaved door at either end. Above were two storeys of fine chambers reached by spiral stairs in round turrets on the west corners and served by latrines where the curtain walls adjoined. The excavations have now revealed the bases of the south tower and the curtains on either side of it, that on the west extending to another D-shaped tower in the middle of the SW side. The remains of a building against the SW curtain and of a hall block between the gatehouse and south tower have also been found. The hall measured 15m by 6m and had a fireplace in the curtain wall. In the 17th century its west wall was mostly removed and a new wall built, halving the width of the building. The excavations also found evidence that the SW side of the inner ward and its towers may have been added as part of a revised plan after the 1282 attack and that the ward was originally larger, extending on this side to the line of the present outer wall.

The last remains of the town walls were removed in the 19th century. They ran from the castle along the shore to a point near the library and then followed a curve defined now by Baker St, Chalbeate St, and Mill St, to the River Rheidol, and then back along the river bank to the castle. One gate faced the river at the bottom of Bridge St. The Great Dark Gate lay in the street of that name, whilst Little Dark Gate lay at the bottom of Eastgate St. The footings of a wall 1.8m thick found in South Road in 1955 were probably part of the defences of the harbour on the south side.

ALLT Y FERIN   SN 522233

The castle of Dinweiler mentioned in Welsh chronicles may have been on this site or at Pencader. A strong promontory 100m long by 60m wide high above the Cothi River is defended on the accessible NE side by a motte 9m high at the east end of a rampart 3m high with a ditch in front. Another ditch cuts off the tip of the promontory.

CARDIGAN   SN 178459   V

The castle of Aberteifi built in 1093 by Roger de Montgomery was probably the ringwork at Dingeraint. A new castle was built in 1110 by Gilbert de Clare. It seems to have held out against a Welsh attack in 1136 and was repaired in 1159 by Roger de Clare, only to be destroyed by Rhys ap Gruffydd in 1165. The new stone castle built by Rhys in 1171 was perhaps on the present site. In 1176 it was the scene of the first Welsh Eisteddfod..."at Christmas in that year the Lord Rhys ap Gruffydd held court in splendour at Cardigan, in the castle. And he set two kinds of contests there, one between bards and poets, another between harpists and crowders and pipers and various classes of music craft. And he had two chairs set for the victors. And he honoured those with ample gifts". After Rhys died in 1197 his younger son Maelgwyn seized the castle and sold it in 1200 to King John, who had it repaired in 1204. The castle was captured in 1215 by Llywelyn ab Iorwerth and was then granted to Rhys Ieuanc. In 1223 William the Marshal the Younger arrived from Ireland with a large fleet and induced the castle garrison to surrender. Maelgwm Ieuanc besieged the castle in 1231 and captured it after the walls were breached by catapults. The existing circuit of much-patched retaining walls enclosing a very overgrown oval court about 90m long by 47m wide are assumed to date from a rebuilding begun in 1240 by Walter Marshal and continued by Robert Waleran, who was granted custody of the castle after Gilbert Marshal died in 1241. Robert also erected the now-destroyed town walls. The castle was later used as an administrative centre by the Crown but decayed early. It was taken by storm in 1644. On the town side of the decayed Georgian house in the NE end of the court is a tower 11m in diameter externally. Although sometimes described as a round keep of c1240 the building is rectangular inside and rises from a square base with spurs. It is more likely to have been the western tower of a twin-towered gatehouse of c1280-1300. There are two smaller D-shaped towers on the SE side of the court. An old engraving shows the eastern tower with spurs.

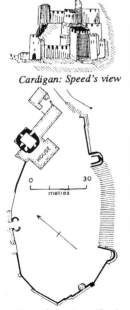

Cardigan: Speed's view

Plan of Cardigan Castle

Cardigan Castle

Gatehouse at Carmarthen

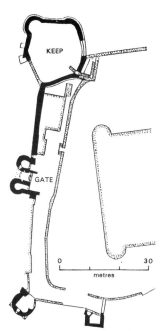

Plan of Carmarthen Castle

CARMARTHEN   SN 413200   V

The castle of Rhyd Y Gors established by William fitz Baldwin in 1093 is thought to have stood to the SW of the present town of Carmarthen. It held out against the Welsh attack of 1094 but was abandoned when fitz Baldwin died in 1096. His successor Richard reoccupied it in 1105 but it was superseded by a new castle at Carmarthen built on Henry I's orders c1109 and the site appears to have been destroyed by the construction of a railway in 1852.

In 1116 Gruffydd ap Rhys made a surprise night attack on the new castle at Carmarthen. It appears that the wooden keep on the motte held out although the bailey was occupied and damaged and the constable Owain ap Caradog was killed. The castle was captured and burnt by Owain ap Gwynedd in 1137, but it was rebuilt in 1145 by Gilbert de Clare, Earl of Pembroke, only to be stormed by Cadell ap Gruffydd and Hywel ab Owain in 1146. This time the Welsh occupied and repaired the castle, and held it against an attack by William fitz Gilbert. It was surrendered to Henry II in 1158 and in 1159 The Lord Rhys tried to take it back but a large army sent to relieve it drove him off. The earliest stonework on the site may date from 1181-3 when Henry II spent £170 on strengthening it. The Lord Rhys attacked Carmarthen again in 1189 after Henry II's death, and in 1196 he burnt the town, although the castle again held out. Llywelyn ab Iorwerth captured and burnt the castle in 1215 after a siege lasting five days. In 1218 the young Henry III granted Carmarthen to Llywelyn under the terms of a treaty but in 1223 William Marshal the Younger forcibly reoccupied the castle and rebuilt and strengthened it. It was back in Crown hands by 1226 and from 1229 to 1232 was held by Hubert de Burgh, Earl of Essex, after which it was given to Gilbert Marshal. In 1233 the castle successfully defied for three months an attack by the Welsh in conjunction with Gilbert's own brother Richard.

After Gilbert was killed in 1241 the castle passed to Robert Waleran. In 1254 it went to Prince Edward. He transferred it to his younger brother Edmund but the castle was obtained back by the Crown in 1279 to serve as the administrative centre of the shire of Carmarthen. It was kept in repair, £380 being spent on making good damage caused by the Owain Glyndwr's forces after it was recaptured from them in 1409. Nearly £100 was spent on the present gateway. In 1469 the castle was captured and briefly occupied by Henry and Morgan ap Thomas in the Lancastrian interest. In the Civil War Carmarthen was initially held by Parliament but was captured by the Royalists, only to be recaptured by General Laugharne. It was then slighted and in 1660 it was described as "quite demolished". Much of what remained was removed in 1789 when a new county gaol designed by John Nash was erected on the site. This in turn was demolished and replaced by the present county council offices in 1938.

The offices lie in the middle of what was the castle enclosure. The impressive retaining walls to the south and east are modern constructions on the line of the former defences. On the south side is the stump of the square Water Tower. At the SW corner stands a round tower about 8m in diameter with pyramidal spurs. Modern buildings have replaced the curtain between the tower and the gatehouse in the middle of the west side. This structure of c1409-13 has two round towers about 5m in diameter flanking a passageway. A four-centred arch connects the towers over the outer part of the passage, and at the top, where there are remains of a corbelled parapet, three bold and wide machicolations project still further. An original length of curtain connects the gatehouse to the shell keep in the NW corner. Not far east of the curtain is a second wall on the same height, but thinner, built in the 1790s to enclose the prison yard. The keep measured about 17m across within walls revetting the upper part of the mound. There are shallow round projections at the two northern corners, and a square forebuilding on the east. The walls stand 1.5m above the mound summit where they are 1m thick, except for some rebuilt parts which are thinner.

Although some earthworks of the Civil War period remain, there are otherwise no significant remains of the town walls enclosing a square area extending from the castle NE side almost to St Peter's Church, facing which were two gateways. A second more irregularly shaped enclosure west of the castle with two gateways facing the river probably originally served as the castle outer bailey.

Machicolation slots on the gatehouse at Carmarthen

CARREG CENNEN   SN 667192   C

This superb site, a limestone crag overlooking a drop of 85m to the River Cennen, was probably occupied in Roman times. Rhys Fychan, son of the Lord Rhys, had a castle here in the early 13th century. His mother Matilda de Braose handed it over to the English when she was at feud with her son, but Rhys recovered it in 1248. He was ejected from his estates by his uncle Maredudd with help from Llywelyn ap Gruffydd in 1257. Carreg Cennen fell to Edward I's forces in 1277, was briefly recaptured during the rising of 1282, and then was given to John Giffard. In 1286-7 the castle was occupied by Rhys ap Maredudd and after recapture was placed in the custody of the Earl of Hereford until 1289. It was then returned to John Giffard, who is thought to have built the existing inner ward before his death c1299, whilst the outer ward is likely to have been added by his son John. The latter was executed by Edward II in 1321, and Carreg Cennen handed over to Hugh Despenser, whose behaviour had caused Giffard and other Marcher barons to revolt. Despenser was himself executed by Queen Isabella and her lover Roger Mortimer when they seized power in 1326.

In 1340 the castle passed to Henry, Earl of Derby, later Duke of Lancaster. It passed via his heiress to John of Gaunt in 1362, and became Crown property when their son became Henry IV in 1399. The castle was captured c1403 by Owain Glyndwr and an account of 1416 refers to repairs to the walls "lately completely destroyed and thrown down by the rebels". After the Yorkist victory at Mortimer's Cross, Thomas and Owain, sons of Gruffudd ap Nicholas, took refuge in the castle and used it as a base for raids on the surrounding countryside. They surrendered to a Yorkist army led by Sir Richard Herbert and Sir Roger Vaughan in the spring of 1462. In August of that year five hundred men equipped with picks and crow-bars were employed to render the castle untenable to save the cost of a garrison, and it was never restored. The estate was given by Henry VII to Sir Rhys ap Thomas and it passed by marriage to the Vaughans of Golden Grove in the late 16th century. In the early 19th century the estate passed to John Campbell, Baron Cawdor, who had the ruin repaired. The castle was handed over to the State for preservation in 1932.

West front of Carreg Cennen Castle

Carreg Cennen Castle

OUTER WARD

GATEWAY

GATE

HALL
ABOVE

INNER
WARD

0   20

Plan of Carreg Cennen Castle

Carreg Cennan Castle

The inner ward of the 1290s is protected by the precipice to the river on the south and rock-cut ditches to the west and north. It measures 32m east-west by a maximum of 28m wide and is enclosed by walls up to 2.8m thick on the vulnerable east and north sides. The thinner west and south walls may incorporate older work from when the site was fortified by the Welsh probably c1220-40. The south wall and the adjacent part of the west wall stand fairly complete. The crossloop in the part of the west wall standing high up must have been served by a timber gallery reached by ladders. The south wall is corbelled out high up to obtain enough width for the wall-walk and parapet. There is a shallow round projection towards the south at the SW corner. At the NW corner is a round tower 8m in diameter. The lowest storey is polygonal inside towards the field and has three loops, one of which has been blocked and a gunport made in the embrasure to cover the west wall, probably in the 1450s. The NE tower is a square of 9m with the corners cambered off with pyramidal spurs. Although the tower is much ruined parts of it remain three storeys high. The lowest level, originally reached only from above, was vaulted and had a fireplace and latrine. The tower rooms connected with a range of apartments filling the east side of the court. Over a series of storerooms and offices were a kitchen at the north end, a hall reached by outside steps from the court, and a suite of two rooms for the lord, firstly an audience chamber and then a bedroom. The bedroom has a fireplace and windows of two lights with shouldered heads facing the court and the drop to the river. A small square tower projecting from the middle of the east side is solid for two levels, but has at third storey level a tiny chapel reached by stairs from the hall.

In the middle of the north side of the inner ward is the gatehouse, a building 14m wide by 10m deep. Towards the field the gatehouse presents a pair of semi-octagonal towers rising with spurs from square bases. The eastern tower is much broken down. They flanked a central passage once commanded by an external machicolation and closed by a turning bridge requiring inner and outer pits. Towards both the field and court the passage was closed by portcullises with double leaved doors behind them. From the room on the west of side the passage a spiral stair in a square turret projecting towards the court led up to two upper storeys, from each of which there was access to the upper rooms of the NW and NE towers by means of a covered gallery and an open wall-walk above. Not long after being built this small but formidable gatehouse was strengthened by erecting a square tower in front of it with a prison in its basement, below the access ramp to the east which was blocked by two more turning bridges with pairs of pits, the outer one commanded by a turret with rounded faces to the north and south. The middle turning bridge was replaced in 1369 when many other repairs to the castle were executed.

Domestic buildings at Carreg Cennen Castle

The early 14th century outer ward sprawling over the gently sloping land to the east and north is roughly a square of 60m. The curtain was 1.7m thick and had solid round turrets at the NW, NE and SW corners and on either side of a gateway on the east side. None of it stands more than 1m high and little remains of the wall south of the outer gate. In the SE quarter is a lime-kiln below which is a long narrow natural cave reached by steps down from the inner ward SW corner and then along a vaulted and loopholed gallery with nesting holes for pigeons built on the edge of the cliff. This whole arrangement probably served little purpose other than to deny the use of the cave to an enemy. The cave has a water supply at its end but it is inadequate for the garrison's needs. Most of the water they needed was provided by rainwater from the roofs collected in a pair of cisterns on either side of the inner gatehouse.

CASTELL GWALTER   SN 622868

This may be the castle of Penweddig mentioned in 1114. It was destroyed by the Welsh in 1136. It was attacked unsuccessfully in 1151 during the course of a quarrel amongst the Welsh themselves but was taken in 1153. The motte rises 4.5m from a rock-cut ditch with a scrub-covered counterscarp bank. A bailey extends for over 40m from the bank to the edge of the gorge of a stream to the north. The big area to the east of of both the motte and the bailey, extending to the edge of steep east slope to the valley below, seems to have formed a weakly defended outer bailey.

CASTELL HUMFREY   SN 441476

The end of a ridge above the Clettwr valley has been cut off by a ditch to make a motte about 6m high and 15m across on top. The summit is not level but has collapsed towards the approach. The castle here existed by 1137 when it was captured and burnt by the sons of Gruffydd ap Cynan. Hywel ab Owain rebuilt the castle in 1151 but in 1158 it was captured by Roger de Clare. However that same year Einion ab Anarawd, a nephew of The Lord Rhys, "eager to abolish his peoples bondage, made for Humfrey's castle, and he slew the knights and other keepers who were there, and won huge spoils and steeds and armour".

Dinefwr Castle

DINEFWR   SN 611217   C

Dinefwr was the seat of the Princes of Deheubarth and has a splendid hill-top site above the Twyi valley. The inner ward walls may date from the time of the Lord Rhys, upon whose death in 1197 the castle was briefly occupied by the English. In 1213 the castle was captured from Rhys Grug by his nephew Rhys Ieuanc aided by an English force "....on the first assault the whole castle was taken, except for the tower. And in that all the garrison gathered together and they defended strongly with missiles and stones and other engines, and from without archers and cross-bow men were shooting missiles, and sappers digging, and armed knights making unbearable assaults, till they were forced before the afternoon to surrender the tower". When Llywelyn ab Iorwerth divided up the Lord Rhys' inheritance at Aberdyfi in 1216, Dinefwr was given to Rhys Grug. Rhys himself dismantled the castle in 1220 to prevent Llywelyn occupying it, but the present keep and the NW tower are thought to have been erected when it was restored not long afterwards. An army of 3,000 men sent by Henry III to reduce the castle in 1257 was destroyed by a series of Welsh attacks.

The castle was surrendered to Edward I during his campaign of 1276-7 against Llywelyn ap Gruffydd and was repaired at a cost of £59. It was briefly held again by the Welsh during the uprising of Rhys ap Maredudd in 1287. In the 1290s Dinefwr was held by John Giffard, who also held Carreg Cennen. In 1317 Dinefwr was granted to Hugh le Despencer and was damaged in the subsequent uprising in protest against the influence at court of the Despencers. The keep was later said to be on the point of collapse and in 1353 £10 was allocated for re-roofing it, although the work was still not executed when the then constable died in 1360. Further damage costing £89 to repair was sustained during Owain Glyndwr's rebellion. In the late 15th century Dinefwr went to Sir Rhys ap Thomas. It was finally abandoned after the mansion of Newtown was built 1km to the north in the 16th century. Conservation and clearance of ivy begun in the mid 1980s is continuing.

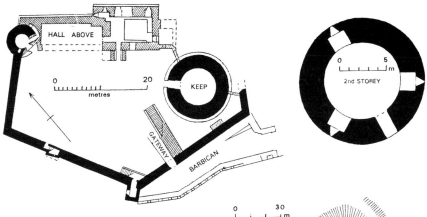

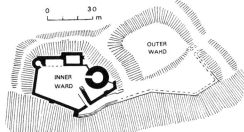

Plans of Dinefwr Castle

The castle can only be reached by a long walk across the estate from the later mansion and then up a steep wooded slope. Slight traces remain of the walls of the outer ward which had a gatehouse on the east side facing a ditch 15m wide. A rock-cut ditch of similar width divided it from the inner ward, which also has ditches to the north and west, whilst the land falls steeply away on the south side.

The single pointed arched gateway on the SE side of the inner ward was approached through a long narrow barbican. The low south wall of the barbican overlooking the drop is fairly complete but not much remains of the rectangular gatehouse through which it was entered on the east. A rectangular turret projecting from an angle of the inner ward closes off the barbican west end. The gateway leads into a pentagonal court about 50m long by 28m wide. The enclosing wall 1.8m thick remains complete on the south, SW, and west sides, and there is a round tower 7m in diameter at the NW corner. The NE corner has gone and thin walls of later date now connect the wall stubs to the keep filling the east end of the court. In the 14th century a domestic range was built up from the steep slope outside the original north wall. The range comprised an upper storey hall (now lacking its south wall) 13m long and 6m wide with a latrine at the west end beside the older round tower (another latrine below is reached from the tower itself), whilst to the east is a block with two storeys of apartments over a basement. The uppermost storey was reached by an open stair from the court. The tower has latrines in a turret at the NW corner and there were smaller rooms in a projection on the east side, now mostly destroyed.

The keep is a very curious building, 13.5m in diameter over walls 2.6m thick above a splayed base with a string course above. Neither the unlit basement reached directly by a door from the court or the room above with three equi-distantly spaced loops which is reached from the battlements of the south curtain by a doorway (now blocked) were habitable rooms. In fact the castle has no real habitable rooms of pre-14th century date, a curious fact considering its early importance, but there were presumably wooden domestic buildings originally. However, it is likely that one or two further levels of the keep were later removed either as a result of damage received in the 1320s or the 1400s, or when a summer-house was built on the top c1675-1740.

Inside the court of Dinefwr Castle

DINIERTH   SN 495624

A wooden castle here was burnt by the sons of Gruffydd ap Cynan in 1136. It was restored by the Welsh but was taken in 1158 by Roger de Clare. A rebuilding begun in 1198 by Gruffydd ap Rhys was only completed in 1203 by his brother Maelgwn, who in 1211 ordered it destroyed to prevent an occupation by Llewelyn ab Iorwerth. The promontory site above the junction of two river valleys 4km east of Aberaeron is naturally very strong and is now very overgrown. The weak east side is defended by a ditch and rampart with a motte at the north end, half of which appears to have fallen into the northern river valley, so that the summit is now very narrow.

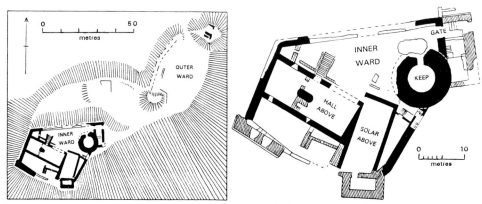

Plans of Dryslwyn Castle

DRYSLWYN   SN 554204   F

Dramatically set on a hill in the middle of the Tywi valley is a castle probably built c1225-45 by one of the Lord Rhys' descendants. It is first mentioned in 1271 when Maredudd ap Rhys died within it. His son Rhys held it against Edward I in 1287. The English managed to undermine the defences but the tunnel collapsed prematurely, burying several attackers. After the castle was captured Alan Plukenet was appointed constable and over £300 spent on repairs, including £109 on a new mill. Dryslwyn was granted to Hugh le Despencer in 1317 and was damaged when neighbouring lords rose in rebellion against Edward II and the hated Despencer favourites. It reverted to the Crown after their fall in 1326. In 1343 a survey reported that £341 was needed to repair the keep and inner ward. Edward III gave custody of the castle to Rhys ap Gruffydd in 1353 on condition that the defences were kept in repair, but after Rhys died in 1356 the Crown had to execute works costing £64. Another Rhys ap Gruffydd in command at Dryslwyn in 1403 sided with Owain Glyndwr, who used the castle as a base for attacks on neighbouring castles. Its later history appears to be unknown.

Until recently all that remained visible of the inner ward was a high fragment of massive masonry containing two window embrasures on the SW side and the outer part of a tower or projection on the south which seems to have contained a chapel on the upper storey, where there are three lancet windows. Excavations have now revealed the lower parts of the rest of the buildings and the stump of a round keep 12m in diameter over walls 3m thick. The inner ward was an irregular hexagon about 30m across with an extension past the north side of the keep to a rectangular gatehouse facing NE. The interior was so filled with buildings that only a small triangular court on the NW and the part by the keep remained unroofed. On the west was a hall block with a central fire set on a pier dividing two chambers below, the largest of of which (to the east) was approached from the small court by a flight of steps. Other chambers lay between the hall block and the SW curtain. The original SW wall was later replaced by the massive walling there still standing high. It was built to replace a section either naturally unstable or destroyed by mining in 1287. East of the hall block was another substantial block of two storeys extending to the chapel tower.

Dryslwyn Castle

Domestic buildings, Dryslwyn Castle

Very little remains exposed of a spacious middle ward 70m long by 30m wide north and NE of the inner ward. Beyond it, to the NW was an outer ward 30m long by 25m wide. A standing fragment containing a passage with steps remains of a tower at the NE end of this ward. West of this fragment lay the outer gate. Parts of the thick west wall of this ward have been exposed, together with slight traces of lean-to buildings.

Keep and domestic buildings, Dryslwyn Castle

GREENCASTLE   SN 396166 & 397162

On a small rocky promontory within a tight bend of the B4312 overlooking the lower reaches of the River Tywi are ivy-mantled ruins of a late medieval house belonging to the Rede family. It was L-planned with a high stair tower set in a NE re-entrant angle between a pair of wings about 18m long, with a gatehouse or porch of which only one side remains in the middle of the west side. The east wing contained a hall over another chamber and has a fireplace breast at the east end. The north wing contained two storeys of rooms over a cellar. Despite its strong site and the probability that at least part of it was embattled, the house itself was not intended to be defensible. It is doubtful if the former court on the west and NW was strong enough to give much protection either. It seems that the name Greencastle (Castell Moel in Welsh) was transferred from the original seat of the estate of Maenor Gain on another, somewhat higher, headland 550m to the south where there are traces of a motte and bailey.

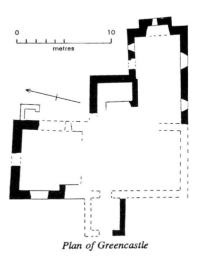

Plan of Greencastle

Greencastle

KIDWELLY   SN 409070   C

Roger, Bishop of Salisbury, built a castle here to command the mouth of the Gwendraeth Fach after being granted an estate here by Henry I in 1106. The hall of the castle is mentioned in a document of c1115. Maurice de Londres is called Lord of Kidwelly in a the record of a battle which he fought with the Welsh nearby at Maes Gwenllian in 1136 but he may not have had possession of the castle there until Bishop Roger died later the same year. The Lord Rhys is said to have built a new castle at Kidwelly in 1190 but it must have fallen to the English by 1201, when Rhys' son Meredith was killed by the castle garrison. Another son, Rhys Grug, captured and burnt the castle in 1215. Rhys Grug relinquished Kidwelly in 1220 but occupied it again during the Welsh rising of 1231, and his son Meredith still held it in 1242. In the meantime the de Londres line ended in an heiress, Hawise, who married firstly Walter de Braose, who died fighting the Welsh in 1233, and then in 1244 Patrick de Chaworth, who in turn died fighting the Welsh in 1258. In the year before his death the castle held out against a Welsh attack, although the town was burnt.

The inner ward of the present castle is thought to have been built by Payn de Chaworth between his return from a crusade in 1274 and his death in 1279. After his brother Patrick died in 1283 Kidwelly and Ogmore passed to the latter's infant daughter Matilda, who married Henry, younger son of Edmund, Earl of Lancaster, brother of Edward I. Henry built the present defences of the outer ward. He later became Earl of Lancaster and his granddaughter Blanche married John of Gaunt, later created Duke of Lancaster. The estate merged with the Crown when their son became Henry IV in 1399. By 1401 King Henry had spent nearly £100 on further work to the still incomplete outer gate. It appears that this gatehouse (possibly then covered with scaffolding and perhaps not fully roofed) was set on fire in 1403 during an attack by Owain Glyndwr troops supported by a French naval force. More than £500 was spent on further work on this building between 1408 and 1422 when it was finally roofed with lead brought over from Bristol. Henry VII granted the castle to Sir Rhys ap Tudor but his grandson was forfeited by Henry VIII in 1531. Later the neglected castle passed to the Earls of Cawdor by whom it was placed in State care in 1927.

Kidwelly Castle

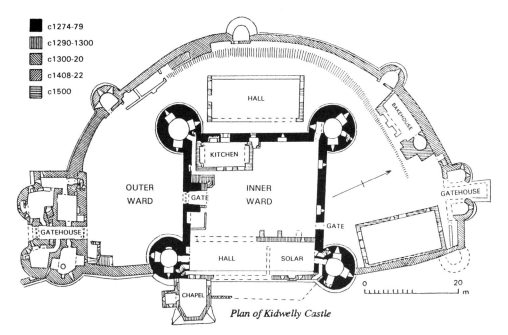

Plan of Kidwelly Castle

The castle consists of a D-shaped outer ward 75m long from north to south by 47m wide surrounding, except on the east where there is a steep drop to the estuary, an inner ward 27m square. The ditch and bank protecting the eastern side are a relic of the castle of 1106-15, whilst a capital of the 1190s built into the later hall shows that the castle was at least partly of stone by 1200. The outer curtain varies in thickness but much of it is about 1.8m wide. Most of it probably dates from the 1320s but may include some late 12th or 13th century stonework and a section on the SW was rebuilt in the 15th century. Three towers, open-gorged as originally built, flanked the western side and there was a gateway on the north with a passage flanked by twin U-shaped towers. The inner parts of this gatehouse are very ruined, and little survives of the central western tower and of another tower at the NE corner, but otherwise the outer defences are fairly complete, including much of the parapets.

A large gatehouse at the south end of the outer ward provided the main entrance into the castle. It is a block measuring 14.4m wide over the D-shaped towers on the south side and 24.3m long over a rectangular projection containing chambers on the west side and a round projection over looking the estuary to the east. The passage was closed by portcullises and doors at either end and was flanked by two rooms on either side. The rooms are mostly of irregular shape and were given vaults in the early 15th century when the stair turret at the NW corner was added, the upper rooms given large new windows facing the court, and the three flat arches with machicolation slots behind then added over the outer gate. Below the outer rooms are vaulted cellars reached from steps down from the entrance passage, so that the outer part of the building has four storeys in all. The storey over the passage contained a central hall with a kitchen on the east, and other rooms to the south and west. The hall was originally reached from the southern room west of the passage but in the 15th century a new outside stair was built alongside the east curtain. The third storey has a similar layout to that below with all the rooms, except the largest, which was a solar, covered with 15th century vaults.

Kidwelly Gatehouse Plan

The gatehouse, Kidwelly Castle

Outer ward, Kidwelly

The inner ward with its modestly sized square plan, four massive drum towers at the corners and simple gateway arches once closed by portcullises has closer parallels of layout in Ireland rather than England and Wales. The towers vary in size from 8.5m to 10m in diameter and each originally had four storeys. When the outer curtain was built earth removed from the older bank was spread over the surface of the outer ward, so that the basements of the western towers, which were reached from above by trap-doors, became subterranean. The towers were then all heightened by one storey, and the original battlements can still be seen embedded in the new walling. Vaults were later inserted in each levels of the SW tower, which was probably then used for keeping documents and valuables. The eastern towers do not project much to the east because of the steep fall of the ground there. They contained three living rooms each with fireplaces over basements reached directly from the outside as built. An eastern domestic range with a solar at the north end and a hall to the south, both set over store-rooms, was built to connect these towers. The lowest living room in the SE tower then became a buttery as the hall screens passage and entrance lay at this end. A passageway from the NE tower led to a 14th century flat narrow area or mantlet east of the hall. At the south end of this mantlet, adjoining the SE tower, and reached from the hall screens passage, lies the chapel, a thinly walled building with a polygonal east end overlooking the estuary. Two other rooms lie below the chapel itself, which has a rib-vaulted sacristy in a square turret on the south side. Tucked between the hall entrance stair and the inner ward main gateway are remains of a small kitchen of c1300. A larger kitchen of c1500 lies on the west side of the court. It served (by means of an original loophole broken out into a doorway) a detached hall of the same date lying beyond in the outer court. Presumably the older hall, of which little now remains, was by then already in ruins. Another large building of about the same period lies between the northern outer gate and the inner ward NE tower.

Kidwelly Castle

Laugharne Castle

LAUGHARNE   SN 303107   V

The castle built by the Taf estuary in the 1090s by Robert Courtemain may have been the earthwork remaining at Llandeilo Abercowin and it is not known when the rock at Laugharne was first fortified. In 1116 the original fortress, then called Abercofwy, was entrusted by Henry I to Bleddyn ap Cedifor. It was held by the Lord Rhys in 1189 and was destroyed but subsequently rebuilt. The large outer ward of the present castle was probably built by Sir Guy de Brian c1280 but one or both of the inner ward round towers may be older work of c1225-45. In the late 16th century Sir John Perrot remodelled the buildings of the inner ward and created a formal garden in the outer ward. After his attainder and death the castle changed hands several times and was illegally partly dismantled in 1613, repairs being subsequently estimated by the Court of Exchequer to cost £2,000. They were never properly implemented and the castle was finally wrecked when it was besieged by Parlimentary forces during the Civil War.

The NW tower of the inner ward probably once formed a keep. It is 10m in diamter over walls 3.4m thick at the level of a basement partly below the court. There are saucer-shaped vaults over the two lowest levels and the lofty storey above has a pointed vault rising from a series of pendentive arches to a point high above the battlements. The NE tower is 8.9m in diameter over walls 2.5m thick. It has no vaults or features of interest. The thinly walled range replacing the original thick curtain between the towers must be of Sir John Perrot's time. It has a D-shaped staircase tower on the north side and contained two storeys of apartments over a dark basement. The court measures about 25m across and has on the west a gatehouse with two round turrets and on the south high outer walls rising from a low cliff with a round turret at the SW corner. Between it and the gatehouse are remains of the kitchen fireplace. These parts appear to be mostly 16th century work. Recent excavations have revealed foundations of the timber framed inner walls of the hall on the south side, where a fine fireplace and two large openings remain in the outer wall. Also revealed is the base of the fountain which Sir John Perrot erected in the court. The outer ward is lozenge shaped, being 80m long by 50m wide. The walls enclosing it have been much rebuilt and no flanking towers remain, although such might be expected at the acute east and west corners. However, there is a gazebo of late date on the SE side, and on the north is a gatehouse with twin semi-octagonal towers and having an upper storey reached by a stair against the east side.

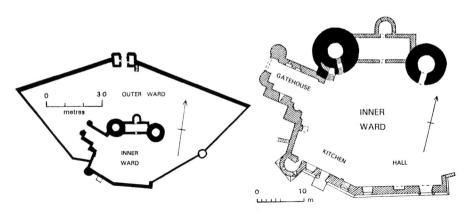

Plans of Laugharne Castle

The part of the town of Laugharne north of the castle was formerly enclosed by a ditch and rampart with a palisade. There is no evidence of a stone wall although it appears that there was once a stone gatehouse at the north end of the main street.

Laugharne Castle

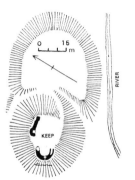

Llandovery Castle

Plans of Llandovery Castle

LLANDOVERY   SN 767343

The motte and heart-shaped bailey erected by Richard Fitz Pons in 1116 beside the River Bran are well preserved. The Welsh burnt the bailey the same year and in 1158 raids by the then owner, Walter Clifford, against Welsh territories precipitated a retaliatory attack in which the whole castle was captured and destroyed. Henry II had the castle repaired and garrisoned in 1160-2. Rhys Grug "subdued" the castle in 1210 after coming to terms with King John. In 1213 John turned against Rhys Gryg and supported the claim of Rhys Ieuanc to Llandovery and Dinefwr. Another relative, Maelgwn, received Llandovery in the division of the Lord Rhys' lands by Llywelyn ab Iorwerth in 1216, but it was possessed by Rhys Grug in 1227, when he was captured by his own son and only released when the castle was surrendered. It was ordered to be garrisoned against Owain Glyndwr in 1403 but was then allowed to decay.

There is no sign that the bailey was ever walled in stone. The motte has fragments of a building of unusual shape built in 1282 by John Giffard. At the west end is a D-shaped tower measuring 10.5m in diameter above a sloping plinth. The room at motte-top level has remains of a loop facing SW. The upper room has a window embrasure above the loop and and jambs of two others, with a latrine leading off from that on the south. It is uncertain whether rest of the motte top was roofed over or formed a tiny open court. On the north side is a small round tower with a square interior enclosing a well and a length of thick walling extending to the east.

Llandovery Castle

LLANEGWAD   SN 517214

The tree-clad motte of Pen y Cnap near the church is site of the "castle of Llanegwad" captured by Rhys Ieuanc in 1203. The mound rises 8m to a summit 15m across and has traces of much later stonework on the south side. The encircling ditch remains now only on the north side. There are traces of a bailey 60m long by 45m wide.

LLANELLI   SN 501004

A motte and bailey within a bend of the River Lliedi, and once the caput of the commote of Carnwyllion, was nearly submerged in the 19th century by a reservoir built to serve a tinplate works. Only the scrub covered top of the 6m high motte remains visible. The castle was captured in 1215 by Rhys Grug. A rectangular moated enclosure, probably medieval but possibly Roman, lay between what are now John Street and Murray Street.

LLANRHYSTUD   SN 552695

On a hill rising 130m above the valleys of the Afon Wyre and Afon Fach which meet at the village of Llanrhystud is an earthwork called Caer Penrhos. The main enclosure 240m long by 120m wide is likely to be Iron Age in date, but probably remained in use as an outer court serving a ringwork on the east side which rises up to 7m above its ditch and 2m above an interior measuring about 45m across. This part was built in 1144 by Cadwaladr, brother of Owain Gwynedd, and was given to his son Cadfan, but in 1150 was captured by Owain's son Hywell. The Lord Rhys captured the castle after a long siege in 1151, but soon afterwards Hywell returned and retook the castle, which was burnt and its garrison slain. The site must have been refortified by Rhys since it was captured from him in 1158 by Roger de Clare. It is assumed to have been recaptured and burnt by Rhys soon afterwards and it was probably then abandoned.

LLANSTEFFAN   SN 351101   C

A castle on this splendid headland site above the Tywi estuary is first mentioned in 1146 when it was captured from the English by the princes Cadell, Maredudd, and Rhys. Maredudd held the castle against an attempt to retake it, the attackers' scaling ladders being thrown down into the ditch, and it was not until c1158 that the Welsh lost control of the castle and surrounding district. In the late 12th century it was held by Geoffrey Marmion and then passed via his daughter Albreda to William de Camville, a Devonshire knight. After Henry II died in 1189 the Lord Rhys broke his peace with the English Crown and captured Llansteffan. William de Camville had recovered it by 1192 when he borrowed money from the Sheriff of Gloucester to refortify the castle, probably with the thin stone wall which surrounds the inner ward. The inner gatehouse was probably added after Geoffrey de Camville recovered the castle following its capture by Llywelyn ab Iorwerth in 1215. The Welsh again captured the castle in 1257 after it and other castles were largely denuded of their garrisons to make up an army to attack Dinefwr and were thus left defenceless when the army was destroyed at the Coed Llathen by a Welsh force led by Maredudd ab Owain and Maredudd ap Rhys.

The second Geoffrey de Camville greatly strengthened the castle in the 1270s and 80s by walling in the outer ward and providing it with a strong gatehouse and towers. When his son William died in 1338 Llansteffan passed by marriage to Richard de Penres or Penrice. In 1367 Edward III ordered Robert de Penres to repair the castles of Penrice and Llansteffan and sent Rhys ap Griffith to oversee the work. Robert was forfeited in 1377 after being convicted of murdering a woman at Llansteffan in 1370, and from then until his attainder and execution in 1388 Llansteffan was held by Sir Simon Burley, Tutor to Richard II. During the Glyndwr rebellion the castle was occupied by Sir John de Penres, Lord of Oxwich, and in 1403 Henry IV granted it to him for life as a reward for recapturing it from the rebels, although it appears the Gwyn family also had some interest in it until in 1416 Llansteffan was handed over to Humphrey, Duke of Gloucester. Subsequently the castle was held by William de la Pole (murdered in 1450), Henry VI's consort Queen Margaret, William Herbert, Earl of Pembroke, Edward (the elder of the two Princes in The Tower), and Jasper Tudor, Earl of Pembroke. They were all absentee lords, except perhaps the latter, for whom the original outer gateway was blocked to make a private residence of the gatehouse, and a new gatehouse was built alongside. In later years a farm lay within the ruined walls and in 1959 Major Fisher-Hoch of Plas handed it over to the State for preservation.

Gatehouse, Llansteffan

Tower of the outer ward, Llansteffan

Gatehouse, Llansteffan

The castle lies 45m above sea level and has steep slopes away from the walls on all sides except to the west where is a double ditch system. The whole enclosed area is D-shaped and about 90m long from east to west by 60m wide. The upper ward represents the original ring-work and is a pentagon of about 45m by 33m defended by a retaining wall just 1m thick which stands up to 4m above the ground outside but rather less above the court. The wall is nearly complete on the west where it has been strengthened and heightened by building a series of arched recesses against it, but is reduced to foundations on the east and south. Excavations on the east side a few years ago revealed the footings of a round tower of the 1230s or 40s measuring about 6m across, plus remains of various domestic buildings mostly built after the time when the upper ward ceased to be regarded as a separate defensive enclosure. The inner gatehouse is about 6.5m square and has an unvaulted passage formerly closed by a portcullis and two sets of doors. The two upper storeys are connected by a stair in the SE corner rising from the jamb of a doorway opening onto the former wall-walk of the curtain on the east side. Parts of the parapet on a corbel table remain.

The walls of the lower ward are 1.8m thick and mostly still stand on average 6m high to wall-walk level, only the parapets being lost. There are D-shaped flanking towers of about 7.5m and 8m in diameter respectively facing NW and NE. At the east corner is an angular bastion, actually no more than an external thickening of the walls, allowing internal recesses at ground level, and latrines above reached by a spiral stair to the wall-walk and a passage. A roof mark on the bastion suggests that the main hall lay along the curtain between it and the NE tower, but a late 15th or 16th century barn now lies on this site. The NE tower contained two upper storeys of pleasant living rooms for the lord over a basement with a single loop. The living rooms have fireplaces and windows facing SW to the court and NE to the sea. The straight sides of the tower are flanked by turrets, that on the east containing a staircase, whilst that on the west contains latrines. The much more ruinous NW tower contains a basement with a loop towards the field and a single upper room with a fireplace on the north and a corbelled out latrine on the south plus two crossloops to the field.

The chief feature of the ruins is the outer gatehouse, a three storied building 17m long and 10.5m wide over the pair of rounded outer faces flanking the former gateway on the north side. The passageway, blocked at both ends c1490, and the flanking guard rooms are all vaulted. Rebuilding in subsequent periods has removed the loops commanding the passage from the guard rooms, and the insertion of an access hatch in the vault has caused part of it to collapse, but two sets of five murder holes commanding the passage still remain. Originally there would have been two portcullises, each with a pair of doors behind them, but few traces of them survive. A doorway beside the curtain on the west leads into the lower of two large single rooms on the upper storeys. The rooms have rounded recesses on the north containing the remains of arrow loops with bottom roundels whilst the south wall facing the court contained fireplaces flanked by fine windows in big embrasures. Spiral stairs connecting these rooms and also serving the former battlements lie in round turrets on the south corners. The stairs do not continue downwards so there was no access between the upper rooms and the guard rooms, the latter only being reached from the passage. The top room had a slot in the outer wall face above the outer gateway arch. Reached from the SE stair are latrine chambers set at intermediate levels in the east wall, here thickened to contain them. When the gateway was blocked a square two storey building containing a new passage closed simply by a pair of doors, and defended only by a machicolation slot, was added immediately to the east.

Llansteffan Castle

Gatehouse, Llansteffan

Inner gatehouse, Llansteffan

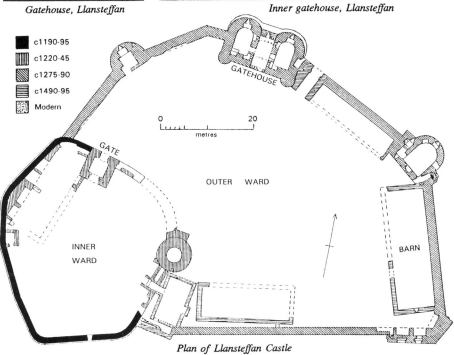

Plan of Llansteffan Castle

NEWCASTLE EMLYN   SN 311407   F

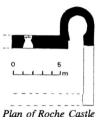

Plan of Roche Castle

Henry III divided the district of Emlyn between Walter Marshall and Maredudd ap Rhys c1240, using the River Cych as a dividing line. Maredudd then built a "new castle" on a ridge within a bend of the Teifi close to the already existing village and motte of Adpar. Edward I took over the castle after the rebellion of Rhys ap Maredudd in 1284 and Edward II had a new hall built for £50 in 1312, but the building soon became decayed, and one report mentions the drawbridge as too weak to take the weight of a horse. Owain Glyndwr damaged the castle, then in private hands, in the early 1400s. In the late 15th century the castle was acquired by Sir Rhys ap Thomas and remodelled as a country residence. It was held for the King in the Civil War but was captured and slighted by the Parliamentarians in 1644.

Only footings, some exposed and some buried, remain of the original 13th century curtain wall around a pear-shaped court about 35m long by 25m wide. Humps indicate footings of domestic buildings on the south side. In the early 14th century the west side was remodelled with a tower added at the SW corner and a gatehouse further north. Parts of both these still stand two storeys high. There are wide window openings probably of late 15th or 16th century date on the gatehouse upper storey and narrower ones below. The building measures 16.8m by 11.5m and has semi-octagonal ended towers flanking a passage probably closed by two sets of doors but with no sign of a portcullis or drawbridge. On the north and south of the court the ground sloped down moderately steeply to the river. Towards the town to the west extended an outer bailey 30m wide by 60m long which was probably never walled in stone. The earthwork occupying the east half of the outer ward so as to help defend the inner gate is a ravelin or bastion of the Civil War period.

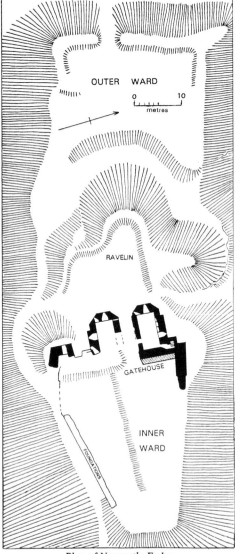

Plan of Newcastle Emlyn

Newcastle Emlyn

ROCHE   SN 294102   V

Beside a bungalow less than 1km south of Laugharne and visible from a path passing close by is a fragment of a 13th or 14th century block having a round turret on one corner and once containing a hall over a vaulted basement. There is thought to have been a stair turret on the south corner. The building lay in a walled court surrounded by a wet moat filled from the stream with still bounds the south and east sides. The de la Rupe family are thought to have owned Roche in the mid 13th century and it was granted to Sir John Perrot in 1575.

Roche Castle

Motte at St Clears

Plan of Ystrad Meurig Castle

ST CLEARS   SN 281154   F

East of the village and on the west bank of the Cynin near its confluence with the Taf lies Banc Y Beili, an earthwork comprising a 6m high mound and a bailey roughly 48m square. There are signs of former stone walls and there is mention of them in the Brut chronicle. The castle was captured and destroyed by The Lord Rhys in 1153. It was rebuilt but again fell to Rhys in 1189, and 1215 it was taken by Llywelyn ab Iorwerth. Giraldus Cambrensis tells us that archers from the Norman garrison were ordered to join Richard I's crusade as a penance for killing a Welsh youth. The site remained in use as late as 1405 when it was besieged by Owain Glyndwr with French help.

Ystrad Meurig Castle

YSTRAD MEURIG   SN 718678 & 702675

The 5m high motte beside the Meurig was built by Gilbert de Clare. Its wooden buildings were destroyed by the Welsh in 1137 but were restored by the sons of Gruffydd ap Rhys. In 1158 Roger de Clare provisioned this stronghold before moving on to recapture the castles of Dinierth, Llanrhystud and Humfrey's. On Christmas Eve 1193 "the war band of Maelgwyn ap Rhys manfully breached the castle of Ystrad Meurig with slings and catapults". In 1195 The Lord Rhys imprisoned his sons Rhys and Maredudd here. Maelgwyn burnt the castle to prevent it being occupied by Llywelyn ab Iorwerth in 1208. The large tree-clad earthwork with buried footings of a substantial rectangular tower on the ridge SW of the church is a relic of a later castle probably built c1220-40 by one of the sons of Gruffydd ap Rhys, to whom Llywelyn gave the surrounding lands, but probably abandoned by the 1270s if not earlier.

YSTRAD PEITHYL   SN 653824

In 1116 the wooden tower on this motte 8km east of Aberystwyth was captured and burnt by the Welsh and its garrison slain. It belonged to Ralf, constable of the castle at Aberystwyth, who had his revenge the following day when the Welsh attacked that castle without knowing Ralf's force had been reinforced from the neighbouring garrisons and were totally defeated. The motte rises 5m to a summit 10m across which has collapsed towards the north. The ditch has an outer bank to the east and south.

CASTELL GWALTER

ABERYSTWYTH

YSTRAD PEITHYL

LLANRHYSTUD

YSTRAD MEURIG

DINIERTH

CASTELL HUMPHREY

CARDIGAN

NEWCASTLE EMLYN

LLANDOVERY

■ STONE BUILDINGS
✳ EARTHWORKS
☐ WALLED TOWNS

ALLT Y FERIN   DINEFWR

CARMARTHEN   DRYSLWYN   CARREG CENNAN

ST CLEARS   GREENCASTLE   LLANEGWAD

LLANSTEFFAN

LAUGHARNE

ROCHE   KIDWELLY

LLANELLI

MAP OF CASTLES
IN CARMARTHEN
AND CEREDIGION

OTHER CASTLES IN CARMARTHEN & CEREDIGION (CARDIGAN)

ABERAERON (Castell Cadwgan) SN 460634 approx Site now fallen into the sea.

ABEREINION SN 686969 Motte (Domen Castell) by confluence of Einion and Dyfi. Probably the castle Aberdyfi burnt in 1156 and rebuilt by the English in 1158.

ADPAR SN 309409 Remains of motte in village north of Teifi at Newcastle Emlyn.

AMMANFORD SN 624125 Motte rising 6m to dished top 19m across in ground of Tir-Y-Dail House. Traces of narrow bailey to north.

BANC Y BETTWS SN 458155 Motte rising 9m to depressed top 16m across. The ditch is cut through rock on the south. It is filled in on the north.

BWLCH Y DOMEN SN 325370 Motte with wet ditch near Penboyr.

CAERWEDROS SN 376557 Motte with high counterscarp to ditch. Captured in 1136.

CASTELL BACH SN 247275 Motte 12m high above Afon Sien. Traces of ditch.

CASTELL COSSAN SN 202268 Mound rising 3.5m to summit 5m across.

CASTELL DU SN 437341 Motte rising 4.5m to summit 7m across. Ditch on NE.

CASTELL DU SN 533472 No traces of former castle near Llanwnen.

CASTELL GWITHIAN (Blaenporth) SN 266489 Motte and narrow bailey with large outer bailey surrounded by streams. Outer rampart removed. Captured in 1116.

CASTELL GWYDDGRUG SN 477356 Motte 4.5m high with ditch between it and a bailey to the east measuring 154m by 36m. Now very damaged.

CASTELL NONNI SN 495399 Small overgrown mound with top 15m across.

CASTELL PISTOG SN 382403 Mound by farm high above north bank of Teifi.

CASTELL PRIDD SN 295496 Last remains removed in 1930.

CASTELL Y DOMEN SN 436126 Mound rising 9m to summit 18m across set 37m above the south side of Gwendraeth Fach.

CASTELL Y GARREG SN 572157 A small mound.

CASTELL Y RHINGYLL SN 578148 Only traces of a mound remain.

CENARTH SN 269414 Slight traces of mound on south side of Teifi.

DINGERAINT SN 164464 Ringwork by mouth of Teifi. Predecessor of Cardigan (p17).

DOLAUCOTHI SN 662401 & 663403 Two mounds beside gold mines.

DOL-WLFF SN 520445 Bungalow on site of earthwork removed in 1970s.

EGREMONT SN 094202 Damaged partial ringwork set above a steep slope.

FELIN CWRWS SN 351411 A partial ringwork in woods above a tributary of the Teifi.

GARN FAWR SN 396238 Ringwork 16m in diameter. 5m high above ditch 1m deep.

GLAN MYNYS SN 731326 Low lying motte rising 7m high to summit 15m across.

GWYNIONYDD SN 424420 Very overgrown ringwork above drop to Teifi. Possibly had a small stone keep built c1220 by Maelgwyn Rhys.

LAMPETER SN 579482 The high but damaged motte in the college grounds is probably the castle of Llanstephen captured by Welsh in 1137.

LLANBOIDY SN 219231 Mound rising 6m from filled in ditch to summit 15m across. Bailey to west 42m by 36m with bank 1m high.

LLANDOWROR SN 253147 Motte rising 6m to summit 24m across by Afon Taf.

LLANFIHANGEL ABERCYWYN SN 297136 Oval bailey platform 45m by 27m west of Trefenty Farm with ringwork 23m across and 7.5m high at west end. See p34.

LLANGADOG SN 709276 9m high motte formed over rock outcrop, now covered with trees and scrub, at NE end of bailey platform with farmhouse on NW side. English Crown spent £17 on repairs in 1160. Destroyed by Rhys Grug in 1209.

LLANGLYDWEN SN 177268 Site of motte now removed.

LLANIO SN 661579 Motte above Teifi rising 4m to summit 13m across damaged on NE. Probably the castle of Richard de la Mare destroyed by the Welsh in 1136.

LLANLLWNI SN 474413 Churchyard cuts into west slope of motte rising 9m to summit 15m across perched above 100m drop into gorge of Teifi.

LLWYNBEDW SN 431497 Ditched mound now reduced in height to 3.5m.

LLWYNDYRIS SN 237433 Motte in wood on north side of Teifi.
NANT Y CARAU SN 369421 Slight traces of ringwork near Penrhiwllan.
NANT YR ARIAN SN 688818 Mound in woods by Afon Melindwr destroyed 1840.
PANT GLAS SN 422260 Mound 9m across on top in trees by farm.
PARC Y CASTELL SN 288427 Slight traces of castle near tributary of Teifi.
PENCADER SN 444362 Motte rising 7m from old railway line on west to summit
   22m across. Ditch and remains of bailey to west. Built by Gilbert de Clare in 1145.
PEN CASTELL SN 402379 Tree-clad mound rising 7.5m to top 18m across. Ditch 6m
   wide still partly water filled.
PEN-Y-CASTELL SN 630746 Shovel-shaped court 35m across divided by rock-cut
   ditch from second court to SE measuring 43m by 30 with ditch. Quarried on NW.
   On hill above Llanilar. Possibly the castle fortified by Maelgwn Fychan in 1242.
ST MARY'S SN 344442 Small motte high above a tributary of the Teifi.
TALLEY SN 631334 Motte rising 4.5m to top 7.5m across on isthmus between lakes.
TEMPLE BAR SN 533544 Earthwork in woodland by tributary of Afon Aeron.
TOMENLAWDDOG SN 360362 Mound 10m high in NE corner of D-shaped bailey
   60m wide by Penboyr church has moat & traces of masonry on summit 7m across.
TOMEN RHYD OWEN SN 444447 Overgrown ringwork above the Afon Clettwr.
TREFILAN SN 548572 Traces of former motte by tributary of Afon Aeron.
WAUN TYMPATH SN 466026 Motte rising up to 15m above silted up ditch.
Y PIGWRN SN 820310 A small motte.
YSTUM ENLLI SN 584032 A mound 9m high with a top 12m by 7m and a 30m
   square enclosure with 4m high rampart and ditch and projections on corners away
   from river lie at either end of open side of a loop of the Loughor.

Llandovery Castle

Motte at Castell Du

CASTLES OF PEMBROKESHIRE

AMROTH   SN 163077

The original timber castle of Earwere (the name Amroth is comparatively recent) stood on the small mound which still remains near the church. The estate then belonged to the de Say family but soon passed by marriage to Cadwgan ap Bleddyn. In the 14th century the Elliots built a modest stone castle 450m to the SE, nearer the sea. It was later enveloped by a mansion later replaced by the present structure in the 19th century. The grounds of this building now form a caravan park. Here in 1802, the then owner, Captain James Ackland, entertained Admiral Nelson and Emma Hamilton.

ANGLE   SM 866030   V

Beside the small estuary at Angle stands a ruined tower 5.5m square over walls 1m thick and 10.5m high ending with corbels for machicolations. It contains over a vaulted cellar three upper storeys of living rooms each with a fireplace, one window, several loops, all linked by a spiral stair in a round turret on the NE corner. The tower stood in the SW corner of a stone-lined moated enclosure fed with water from the estuary and there was originally in the NE corner a second tower, also with a vaulted basement which survived into the 20th century. There are also traces of a dovecote. Angle, sometimes called Nangle, was held by a family of that name until it passed to Robert de Shirburn in 1278 when he married their heiress. The Shirburns built the tower sometime in the late 14th or 15th century. Angle later passed to Sir John Perrot, and after his death in 1592 was held successively by Walter Rees, John Kynner, Lord Cawdor, and others. At one time there was an inn within the enclosure, but it later fell into ruin. The estate was sold to John Mirehouse in 1805.

Boulston

Tower House at Angle   *Plans of the tower at Angle*

Benton Castle

Bonville's Castle

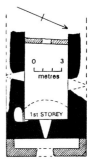

Boulston: plan

BENTON   SN 006068

This castle stands on a rock in a garden above the west shore of the Daugleddau. It may have been built by Bishop Beck of St Davids, d1293, but it is perhaps more likely to be the work of the de la Roches c1235-75. Ernest Pegge began to restore the long neglected ruin in 1932 and placed his own mask in concrete over the entrance on the south side. This entrance pierces a lofty wall 2.7m thick with a parapet on both sides, the only part of the curtain around a tiny court to remain intact and little altered. This wall connects a round tower about 5m in diameter, now much restored, to a higher tower about 7.5m in diameter. The large tower contains three storeys of dark rooms without fireplaces or stairs, although the two upper levels have latrines contained in a square turret on the west side. The battlements at the top, which are partly late 15th century and partly modern, form an octagon. Old drawings show that there was a tower or hall-block on the north side of the court, with a postern adjoining. In front of the entrance a natural outcrop of igneous rock forms a natural barbican.

BONVILLE'S   SN 125052

Nothing now remains of this building near Saundersfoot which is said to have been built in the reign of Edward III by Nicholas de Bonville. From sketches and a description made in the 1860s it seems to have been an embattled block containing a living room over a vaulted cellar and having two or three other vaulted rooms in a wing. There was evidence that a hall block once adjoined one side, making a similar arrangement to that which is assumed at Eastington, except that here the wing rose one stage higher than the main block and additionally contained a spiral stair. After Nicholas' grandson John died probably c1400 the estate is likely to have passed by marriage to the Carews. In 1577 Erasmus Saunders, Mayor of Tenby, was residing in Bonville's Castle. In 1680 William Jones lived in the tower and it appears that this family had obtained it by marrying a Williams' heiress. In 1890 the decayed building was in use as a workshop and stores for the Bonville's Court Colliery. It fell into ruin soon afterwards and was buried under a waste tip, although remains were still visible in 1946.

BOULSTON   SM 981124   V

Hidden in woods by the shore of the Western Cleddau, far from any public road, are ruins of a house of the Wogan family. It was originally a defensible tower or hall block 8.7m wide over walls 2m thick and more than 14m long. In the 16th century it was extended to where a four storey fragment now lies over a stream to the west. The rest was then remodelled above the vaulted cellar. The original SE stair was blocked and the northern of three basement loop embrasures was probably then broken out to give access. New straight stairs connecting three upper storeys were then provided by a small east extension, the lowest flight rising over the stump of the original end wall.

CAREW   SN 045037   O

Carew is said to have formed part of the dowry of Princess Nest, who married Gerald de Windsor in 1100. He is thought to have raised a motte and bailey castle here on a low outcrop beside a tidal creek of the Daugleddau in 1105. The first reference to the "domus de Carrio" is not until 1212 but the old tower adjoining the entrance is probably 12th century work. In the late 13th century it became part of what is now the east range, and shortly afterwards a western range containing a large hall was built, together with massive round towers on its outer corners. It appears that both these ranges were the work of Sir Nicholas Carew, although work on them probably continued after his death in 1311 under his son John. Sir Edmund Carew sold the castle c1480 to Sir Rhys ap Thomas who rebuilt the outer gate and remodelled both ranges, inserting many new mullioned windows. Sir Rhys was one of the leading Welshmen of his day and was high in favour with Henry VII. In 1507 Sir Rhys held a tournament at Carew to celebrate his being made a Knight of the Garter in 1507. The castle reverted to the crown after Henry VIII had Sir Rhys ap Gruffydd (grandson of ap Thomas) executed for treason in 1531. Queen Mary granted the castle in 1558 to John Perrot of Haroldston, reputely a bastard son of Henry VIII, and thus her half-brother. In the 1580s Sir John built the range on the north side of the court in the hope of a prospective visit by Queen Elizabeth I. He is said to have richly furnished the castle with Turkish carpets, Irish rugs, learned books and musical instruments but before he could occupy the castle he was convicted of treason and died attainted in the Tower of London in 1592. The castle was later granted to the Somerset branch of the Carew family, whose successors still own it, although it is leased to the Pembrokeshire Coast National Park Authority. A series of tenants used the lands over the centuries, but the castle ceased to be occupied after the 1680s. At the start of the Civil War the Philipps family of Picton (then tenants) held it for Parliament. A Royalist garrison installed by the Carews in 1644 held out against Parliamentary attacks that year, but in 1645 the castle fell to Colonel John Poyer, only to be recaptured by Colonel Gerard in May. It was finally wrecked soon afterwards when it was assaulted by Colonel Rowland Laugharne and the vulnerable south curtain wall was breached.

South side of Carew Castle

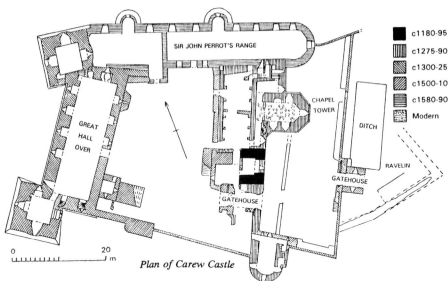

Plan of Carew Castle

Legend:
- c1180-95
- c1275-90
- c1300-25
- c1500-10
- c1580-90
- Modern

The hall block on the west side of the court measures at ground level 25m long by 8m wide within walls up to 3m thick. The hall itself lies on the upper floor and was reached from the court by open steps up to a porch added by Sir Rhys ap Thomas. The shields on it of Henry VII, Prince Arthur and Catherine of Aragon can be precisely dated to the short period when the last two were together in 1500-1. The hall has a magnificent open timber roof within the parapets and was given by Sir Rhys an oriel window facing the court at the north end of the east wall. The round towers adjoining this block are 10.5m in diameter above the massive square bases with tall pyramidal spurs. The base of the SW tower is more or less square to that of the hall block but the base of the NW tower is angled round about 40 degrees. This creates an acute re-entrant angle on the west between the tower base and hall block in which is cunningly concealed a postern, later blocked up. Both towers contain a vaulted basement and two storeys of pleasant private rooms, later given two and three light windows, and have corbelled parapets and the stumps of turrets over the staircases.

The east range contains a lesser hall (covered in 1995 by a scaffold and plastic roof) over a vaulted undercroft. Projecting eastward from this part of the range is a tower with a polygonal east end. At hall level this tower contains a vaulted chapel with a room for the priest contained (along with latrines) in a block between the main range and the north side of the tower. South of the lesser hall is the old tower, a building 7.6m wide but of unknown original length. It originally formed the gateway and has a blocked arch in the east wall. The present entrance lies beyond it to the south and has inner and outer arches, both with provision for a two-leaved door secured with drawbars. The inner arch also has a portcullis groove, and there are three murder holes or machicolations in the passageway vault. Beyond here the range is very ruined. Not much remains of the south curtain wall wrecked during the Civil War and a tower in the middle of the wall which is thought to have contained the kitchen has vanished. However the SE tower stands nearly complete. In order to flank the gateway this tower projected boldly eastward (where it is rectangular and contains latrines), but it also projects from the south front where it presents a semi-circular face. The result is a very unusual piece of planning. This tower is rather less massively built than the Chapel tower and the western towers and also has a parapet of great height above the corbelling. It probably represents an earlier or later campaign of construction.

Outer gatehouse at Carew

Sir John Perrott's range contains chambers with a total length of 46m extending along the north side of the castle beyond the original enclosed area. There were only poorly lighted storerooms on the lowest level, and the large mullioned windows of the two upper storeys are far out of reach of any intending intruders, so the defensive strength of the castle was little compromised by this embattled addition. On the north side are two half-round projections forming bay windows rising from tall and massive battered bases. The eastern two thirds of the uppermost level seems to have been a long gallery typical of great Elizabethan houses.

Beyond the east side of the castle is a low embattled wall enclosing a court about 15m wide. The wall seems to be mostly original work of c1320 but the gatehouse is mostly of the 1490s. It measures 6m long by 5.5m wide and has upper rooms reached by steps on the south side. North of this gatehouse is a stone-lined section of dry moat 18m long by 6.6m wide. Little now remains of a Civil War ravelin built in front of the outer gate, or of a wall built across the outer court in front of the inner gate.

Old postcard of Carew Castle

Inside the court at Carew Castle

Cilgerran Castle

Cilgerran Castle

CILGERRAN   SN 195431   C

It is uncertain when a castle was first established on this superb site on a rock above the gorge of the Teifi. Possibly the castle of Cenarth Bychan "fortified with a ditch and a wall" by Gerald de Windsor in 1108 lay here. In the following year his wife the celebrated beauty Princess Nest and her children were abducted from Cenarth Bychan by a band of Welshmen led by Nest's cousin Owain ap Cadwgan, whilst Gerald only escaped by climbing down a latrine shaft. Cilgerran fell into Welsh hands for a longer spell after a Norman and Flemish army was defeated at Crug Mawr nearby in 1136. Twenty years later Rhys ap Gruffydd submitted to Henry II, but he recaptured Cilgerran in 1165 and a Welsh garrison there twice withstood sieges by Normans from Pembroke in 1166. After Rhys died in 1197 Cilgerran was temporary lost by the Welsh during the bickering between his sons Gruffydd and Maelgwn. In 1204 Cilgerran was captured in a surprise attack by William Marshal, Earl of Pembroke, but Llywelyn ab Iorwerth recaptured it in 1215. The younger William Marshal, 2nd Earl of Pembroke, captured Cilgerran in 1223 with forces brought over from Ireland and the rebuilding of the castle began. In 1257 Llywelyn ap Gruffydd defeated the Normans nearby and attacked the now much-strengthened castle. It was damaged but remained untaken.

After Anselm, the last of the Marshal Earls of Pembroke, died in 1245 Cilgerran passed to his sister Eva. When her daughter's son George Cantilupe died in 1273 the castle went to his sister Joan, married to Henry de Hastings. Their line of descendants died out when John de Hastings, a minor, died in 1389 and Cilgerran was retained by the Crown. The castle was neglected during this period as the heirs were mostly minors who never occupied it. A survey in 1275 noted that 100 marks worth of repairs were needed, and in 1326 the castle was said to be worth nothing as regards rent because it was ruinous. In 1377 the risk of a French invasion coupled with a local uprising under Owain Lawgoch prompted Edward III to have the castle repaired and strengthened. It was damaged during the revolt of Owain Glyndwr but it is uncertain whether his forces ever took possession of it. In later years the lordship of Cilgerran was associated with the Earldom of Pembroke. Henry VII gave custody of the castle to William Vaughan as a reward for aid when Henry was fleeing from Edward IV. The castle does not appear to have been used in the Civil War and by 1685 it had passed to the Pryse family of Gogerddan. It was noted as a scenic ruin in the 18th century, being painted by artists such as Wilson and Turner. In 1863 a considerable section of the eastern wall of the outer ward collapsed as a result of slate quarrying adjacent to the castle. Sir Lewis Pryse sold the ruin in 1938 to Mrs Colby of Ffynhonnau who gave it to the National Trust. It is now maintained by Cadw.

Two low fragments, one on the north side and the other immediately west of the inner gate, remain of the 12th century buildings. They are not enough to indicate the layout at that period, to which may also belong the rock-cut inner ditch. The existing inner ward is a pentagon about 34m across. The shortest side is that to the SE which contains a postern and is flanked by two large drum towers, known as the East Tower and the West Tower. Both are of four storeys and have their internal and external edges set with different centres so that the vulnerable outer parts have more massive walling than the parts facing the court. The east tower is thought to be of c1223-30 and has window embrasures with seats and pairs of crudely made lights facing the court at second and third storey levels, and a fireplace on the topmost storey. The lowest room is entered directly from the court and has two slits flanking the doorway. The upper levels have cross-shaped arrow-loops facing the field. A separate doorway from the court leads onto the foot of a spiral stair to the upper levels. From this stair is reached the wall-walk on the curtain running NE from the tower to a broken off end with a pair of latrine shafts overlooking the cliff edge.

Cilgerran Castle

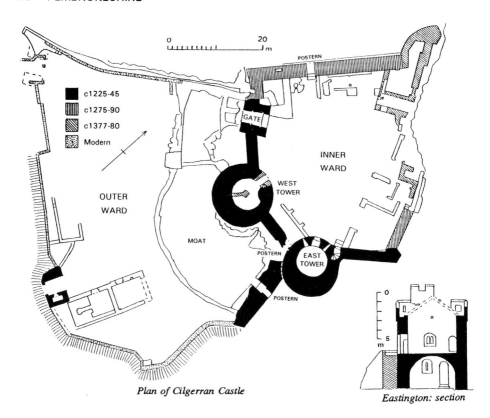

Plan of Cilgerran Castle

Eastington: section

With an external diameter of 11.8m the west tower is the larger of the two. It and the now much ruined rectangular gatehouse beyond to the west were probably built c1235-40. This tower served as a keep and was originally entered by means of an external wooden stair to the second storey. The upper rooms have large windows facing the court but only arrow-slits towards the field. The basement doorway and cross-wall are 14th century alterations. The two upper rooms of the gatehouse, one of which may have been a chapel, seem to have only been reached directly from the keep by means of the wall-walk and a passage below it. The 12th century defences facing the Teifi on the NE and the Plysgog on the NW were replaced by more massive walls in the late 13th century. The NW wall remains intact except for its parapet. It is pierced by a postern and is 3m thick and 3m high towards the court but much higher towards the Plysgog. There are slight remains of a late medieval kitchen built against it. A large U-shaped tower with an angular north end was built at the north corner of the court in the 1370s but not much remains of it. The low walls of minor rooms on the north side of the inner ward are also of that date.

Beyond the ditch to the south and SW lay an outer court with an average width of 27m. The thin walls bounding the outer court are modern. Little remains of its curtain wall except for a thick and lofty section crossing the ditch, from which opens a postern. There is also the base of a tower measuring about 8m by 5m which contained the gateway passage with a tiny room for a porter or guard on the east side. The adjoining bakehouse is much later in date, by which time the gateway had been blocked and a new gatehouse built where the present approach is at the SW corner.

DALE   SM 805059

The manor of Dale was held by the de Vale family, who were established in Pembrokeshire by c1130, as tenants of the barony of Walwyn's Castle. In 1293 Robert de Vale was granted the right to hold a weekly market and annual fair at Dale. When he died in 1303 his estates were divided among his four daughters. Robert may well have had a castle at Dale, but the vaulted rooms remaining in the south wing of the present mansion (which is a private residence) are probably of after his time. It was at Dale that the future Henry VII landed in 1485 and met Sir Rhys ap Thomas. In the 17th century Dale was held by the Walter family, one of whom, Lucy, achieved fame by becoming the mistress of Charles II and bearing him a child who became the ill-fated Duke of Monmouth. When the estate was sold by her brother Richard to David Paynter in 1669 the latter acquired along with the house a portrait of Lucy. Dale passed to William Allen when he married Paynter's daughter in 1699, and it went by marriage in 1776 to the Lloyds of Mabws. They became the Lloyd-Philippses in 1823.

EASTINGTON   SM 901024

This building (originally called Jestynton) probably dates from the second half of the 13th century and was a seat of the Perrots, although only a secondary one after they moved to Haroldston. In the 16th century the estate passed by marriage to the Philipps family and the 17th century it was held by the Meares family, two of whom, William and his brother George were successively made Sheriffs of Pembrokeshire in 1673 and 1692. They lived here until 1842 when John Meares sold the estate to John Mirehouse. The remains consist of a rectangular block 13m long by 7.5m wide and 7.6m high to a wall-walk protected by a loopholed and embattled parapet. It contained just one large living room with a fireplace in the east wall and windows of two lights with trefoiled heads in the north and south end walls above a dark barrel-vaulted basement with three loops and four recesses. There are signs of former upper windows removed by later alteration in the east and west walls. Smaller chambers with pointed tunnel-vaults are contained in a wing projecting 5m from the north end wall. There are separate entrances to each storey, the upper entrance being reached by an outside stair and having from it a stair in the north end wall to the wall-walk. There is no communication between the two storeys. It appears that the building formed a semi-fortified solar block with a hall (now gone) adjoining on the west.

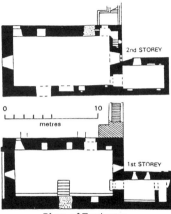

Plans of Eastington

Eastington

HAVERFORDWEST   SM 953157   F

Gilbert de Clare is thought to have founded this castle in the 1120s before he became Earl of Pembroke. It was besieged and captured by Gruffydd ap Rhys after the battle at Cardigan in 1136 but was soon recaptured. Gerald of Wales visited the castle in 1188 and describes an incident in which a robber imprisoned in a tower in the castle was given an indemnity and released after he captured and ransomed the sons of the Earl of Pembroke and Robert fitz Tancred, constable of the castle, when the young boys visited him in his cell. King John stayed at the castle in 1210 whilst returning from Ireland. It held out against attacks by Llywelyn ab Iorwerth in 1220 and Llywelyn ap Gruffydd in 1257, although the surrounding area was devastated on both occasions. Edward I visited the castle in 1284 and shortly afterwards it was rebuilt by Queen Eleanor, who had acquired possession, at a cost of £760.

Haverfordwest Castle

New stables were erected in 1387. An inventory of arms and armour then at the castle includes 2 cannon and 6 hand guns plus a stock of stone balls for them to fire and a barrel of gunpowder. In 1405 the castle held out against an attack by Owain Glyndwr's forces, although the outer gate was badly damaged during the siege. The new tower built in 1407-8 may have been by the outer gate, and at the same time the inner gate was provided with a new drawbridge. In 1479 the sum of £100 was allocated for repairs at the castle but it was probably mostly left to decay. In 1577 Robert Davy refers to "the late inhabited parte of the castle being utterlie decayed as before". The castle was garrisoned for King Charles in the Civil War but in February 1644 Colonel Laugharne managed to take it without a shot being fired when the garrison panicked after Pill Fort was captured. Colonel Gerard recaptured the castle in July but soon afterwards it was again lost without fighting after Laugharne defeated a larger Royalist force travelling from Haverfordwest to Narberth. Cromwell ordered the castle to be destroyed by the local townsfolk in 1648. They found demolishing it hard going and probably all that was done was the removal of the battlements and the wrecking of the inner and outer gatehouses. A range built in the outer ward in 1818 to serve as the county gaol now houses the county museum and archives. From 1879 until 1963 a building in the inner ward served as a police station.

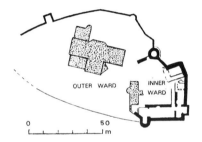

Haverfordwest Castle

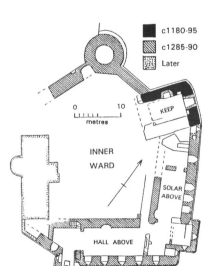

Plans of Haverfordwest Castle

Haverfordwest Castle

View towards the keep, Haverfordwest Castle

The castle consists of a strongly sited inner ward at the east end of a promontory commanding the lowest crossing place of the Western Cleddau, and an outer bailey 70m wide extending 90m towards the west approach. Low retaining walls still mark out the shape of the outer bailey but nothing remains of the outer gateway at the west end, nor much of two round towers and a smaller intermediate turret which flanked the northern side. A gabled building has replaced the westernmost of these towers.

On the east and south sides of the inner ward are remains of two late 13th century ranges of two storeys. Fireplaces in the inner walls, which are now nearly destroyed down to ground level, indicate that the lower rooms were for habitation, not storage. The outer walls stand almost complete and have many loops and windows. The south range contained a hall and has a small round tower at its west end. In the east wall of this tower a straight stair leads down to a postern giving onto what was a terraced garden called the "Queens Arbour". The corner between the ranges has a square projection (with chamfered upper corners) which contained a chapel on the upper level. The east range was presumably the solar block and has large blocked windows on the upper level. In the NE corner are remains of a keep probably of c1180-1210 which is 13m long by 9m wide over walls 2.4m thick. The two walls towards the court are reduced to their footings but the outer walls still stand high. The NE end wall has an unusual curved outer face. The north corner of the court has around tower about 8m in diameter with its interior now inaccessible. This part may be as early as the 1230s. Nothing remains of what is assumed to have been a twin round-towered gatehouse either of the 1230s or 1280s on the west side of the court.

LLAWHADEN   SN 073174   F

Llawhaden belonged to the Bishops of St Davids and was a vulnerable outpost lying on the Landscar or boundary between the England and Welsh parts of Pembrokeshire. The original ringwork is thought to have been erected by Bernard, a chaplain of Queen Matilda, appointed Bishop in 1115. Gerald of Wales visited his uncle, Bishop David Fitzgerald, here in 1175. The castle was captured by the Lord Rhys in 1192 and destroyed by him in the following year. In the 1220s or 30s the castle was rebuilt in stone, and relics of this period are the foundations of a round tower 8m in diameter on the west, and of a second round tower 5.5m in diameter on the NW. These underlie, and therefore must have been superseded by the walls that stand today, probably begun under Bishop Beck in the 1280s, and continued by David Martyn, Bishop from 1293 until 1327. The imposing gatehouse was probably added by Bishop Houghton, who held the see from 1361 until 1389. Bishop John Morgan imprisoned a wicked woman named Tanglost in Llawhaden Castle but she was freed by her friend Thomas Wyriott of Orielton, whose troop of horsemen managed to break in. The castle rapidly deteriorated and was plundered for stone after Bishop Barlow, who held the see from 1536 to 1547 stripped the lead from the roofs and sold the furnishings, supposedly to help provide a dowry for one of his illegitimate daughters. The ruins were handed over to the State by the Welsh Church Committee in 1931.

Llawhaden Castle

A deep dry moat surrounds the castle, which had an open court about 30m across between the ranges surrounding it on all sides. Little remains of the 22m long by 7m wide hall, which lay over the surviving long vaulted cellar in the massively walled NE range probably of the 1280s or 90s. The hall itself was reached by steps up over the lower entrance. At either end of the range are rectangular wings projecting out towards the field. That at the north end contained a kitchen, unusually placed on the upper floor, whilst that to the east contained the solar. The early 14th century SE range contained, over the usual cellars, a set of apartments reached from the court by a stair turret in the middle of that side. The eastern half of the second storey contained a fine chapel 13m long. The outer wall of this range and the polygonal towers at either end stand to full height. Both towers contained vaulted living rooms over an octagonal cellar in the east tower and a rectangular prison in the south tower. The south range contained further apartments with latrines in a rectangular tower at the SW corner, now much broken down. Beyond lay the gateway passage and beyond it was the SE range, which formed quarters for the garrison. The twin-round fronted outer part of the gateway added probably c1380 stands higher than the older work behind it despite being of a more flimsy construction. This frontage contained three storeys and a round arch links the towers below the topmost storey. Very little remains of two further ranges on the west side with a passage to a postern between them. That nearest the kitchen wing was a bakehouse. The other seems to have been of light construction, even towards the field, and was perhaps a later addition. In front of it stands the well.

Llawhaden Castle

The hall block at Llawhaden

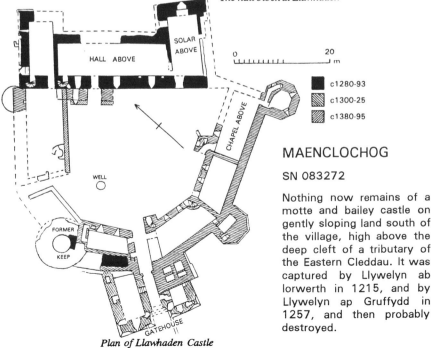

Plan of Llawhaden Castle

Key:
- c1280-93
- c1300-25
- c1380-95

MAENCLOCHOG

SN 083272

Nothing now remains of a motte and bailey castle on gently sloping land south of the village, high above the deep cleft of a tributary of the Eastern Cleddau. It was captured by Llywelyn ab Iorwerth in 1215, and by Llywelyn ap Gruffydd in 1257, and then probably destroyed.

Manorbier Castle

MANORBIER   SS 064978   O

Manorbier was held along with the manors of Penally and Begelly as a barony forming part of the earldom of Pembroke. From the early 12th century until at least the 1360s Manorbier was held by a minor branch of the de Barri family who took their name from Barry in Glamorgan. Its position made it a comparatively safe backwater and there are no records of any attacks upon it by the Welsh. The castle existed in earth and timber form by 1146 when it was the birthplace of Gerald de Barri, later to be the ecclesiastic better known as Geraldus Cambrensis. He was the son of William de Barri and Angharad, daughter of Gerald de Windsor and the celebrated Princess Nest, daughter of Rhys ap Tewdwr. Either William or his successor Philip built the hall house at Manorbier. Certainly it must have been Philip who built the old tower beside the gateway. He held a considerable estate in Ireland and it must have been the proceeds from that, rather than the more modest Pembrokeshire estate, that provided funds for his grandson David to erect the curtain wall during the 1230s or 40s. David was slain in Ireland in 1262 and was succeeded by his son, another David, created Justiciar of Ireland in 1267. Probably it was he who built the chapel block at Manorbier.

The de Barri records for the 14th century are confused and it is difficult to tell who owned or did what. What is clear is that a David de Barri was forcibly ejected from Manorbier by his uncle Richard some time in the 1320s but the rights and wrongs of the complex case in which the Carews were involved are now difficult for us to judge. John de Holland, Duke of Exeter, had a claim to the estate at the time of his forfeiture and execution in 1399, after which Manorbier and Penally were granted to John de Windsor but it seems that John's widow and her second husband Sir John Cornwall remained in possession. The latter was ordered by Henry IV to put Manorbier in a defensible state against Owain Glyndwr in 1403. The Holland titles were restored in 1417 and 1444 but the estates were forfeited to the Crown after Edward IV came to the throne in 1461. In 1484 Richard III entrusted Manorbier and several other castles to Richard Williams in an ill-fated attempt to guard Milford Haven against invasion.

From 1487 until her death in 1509, Manorbier was held by Henry VII's mother Margaret, Countess of Richmond. Henry VIII gave Manorbier to his young bastard son Henry, Duke of Richmond and Somerset but it was leased out and another lease was granted after the Duke died in 1537. In 1601 Thomas Bowen was given a lease of the castle and later his son Charles obtained the freehold. It appears the castle was then ruinous and the court used as pasture. It was surrendered to a Parliamentary force under Rowland Laugharne in 1645 probably without much resistance. In the 1670s Thomas Bowen transferred Manorbier to Sir Erasmus Philipps of Picton Castle as part of a settlement in which the Bowen debts were paid off and he married into the Philipps family. The barn in the outer court was probably built about this time. In the 1880s J R Cobb obtained a lease of the castle and inserted a new house in the NE end of the long barn in the inner ward and also floored and roofed the two round towers and gatehouse. These tower rooms are thought to have been used by soldiers during the first World War, tiny stoves then being inserted to provide some heating.

The castle is strongly and picturesquely sited on a ridge running SW from the village. The hall block at the far end, an embattled and irregularly set-out keep-like building 20m long by 10m wide, is the oldest part. An external stair of much later date rises up to an entrance into the hall in the middle of the north side. Beside the doorway is a fireplace with a later oven and beyond that an original window embrasure. The unlit basement below the hall is now divided into three. The west end of the block was divided off from the beginning, and contained a dark buttery at hall level with a private room above. The chamber has a fireplace and a latrine corbelled out from the west end with a later substructure to enclose a flue.

Manorbier Castle

Manorbier Castle

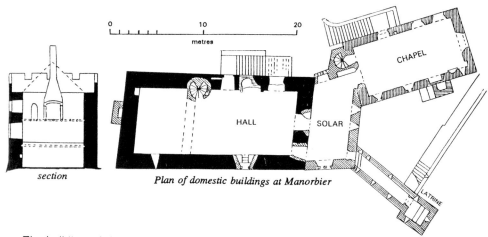

section   *Plan of domestic buildings at Manorbier*

The building of the curtain wall around the spacious inner court 67m long by 44m wide must have stretched the de Barri resources to the limit. The SE wall is 1.6m thick and has a wall-walk 3m above the court but more than 6m above the steeply sloping ground outside where it has a high battered base. The parapet was later heightened as a screen wall with merlons more than 4m above the wall-walk. The north and NW walls meet at a slight angle containing a latrine and from which projects a round bartizan of c1300. Here not only the parapet has been heightened but the main wall as well with a new wall-walk 1.8m above the original one. The more vulnerable walls facing the NE approach have a ditch in front and are flanked by towers 7m in diameter at either end, whilst the gateway, originally just a simple opening, was commanded by the old tower alongside it. This tower was probably built c1200 and measured 7.5m by 6.2m over walls only about 1m thick. On the north and east these have mostly collapsed. The north tower is a D-shaped building originally open to the court unless there was a wooden framed wall across the gorge. A gable surviving from an otherwise vanished 17th century range now closed off the gorge. The SE tower is a full round and has three storeys connected by stairs following the curve of the walls. The parapet of this tower was remodelled during the Civil War period when also a triangular redan was built in front of the gatehouse.

The gatehouse built c1280-1300 contained two rooms over a passage closed by two portcullis. At the same time the curtains were raised, that north of the old tower having a high screen parapet supported by flying arches over the wall-walk, which to the south the original wall-walk 4m above ground became a passage joining the rooms in the gatehouse and SE tower, and a new wall-walk was provided above it.

The chapel added in the 1260s is a fine vaulted room reached by a 16th or 17th century forestair and having three lancets and sedilia in the south wall, a pair of two-light windows facing north, and windows probably of three lights (the tracery has all gone) in the east and west walls. Below is another vaulted room later provided with a large fireplace in the south wall. Soon after the chapel block was completed another block was built between it and the hall. This block contains a chamber at hall level with a vaulted passage above. The top storey formed a new and more comfortable solar than that in the original hall-block. It was reached by a spiral stair rising from the west end of the chapel, which was presumably screened off. Not long afterwards, i.e. c1300, a high screen wall was built between the SE corner of this new block and the SE curtain wall which was originally intended to continue beyond this point to enclose a small space SW of the hall block. The screen wall contains galleries leading from the chamber and solar to latrines a discreet distance away in a turret at the far end.

The vaulted chamber now serving as the shop beside the gate was a guard room probably built at the same time as the curtain walls. The NW curtain has three later embrasures let into it within one of which is built an oven. Other foundations with evidence of a hearth and oven, and the presence of a well, show that the kitchen and bakehouse lay in this position. A fragment also remains of another range further east. On the SE side of the court is a long barn, possibly of c1500. The central part was later made into a residence and windows inserted into the cart-doors. This part is now ruined and the NE end is incorporated into a modern house.

NE of the inner ward is a D-shaped outer court 90m long by 60m wide probably built in the 1260s. Not much remains of the thin wall which enclosed it except on the overgrown north side where there are traces of a small D-shaped tower with an open gorge. In the middle of inner ward end of this court are ruins of a long barn in which is built a modern garage.

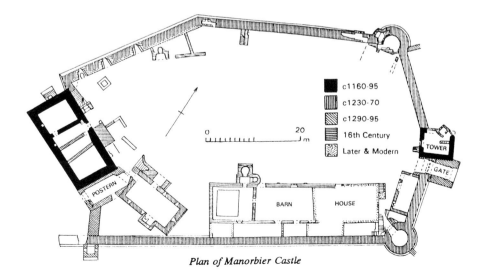

Plan of Manorbier Castle

Narberth Castle

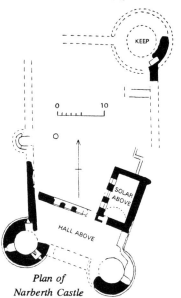

*Plan of
Narberth Castle*

SE tower at Narberth

NARBERTH   SN 109143   F

The castle of Arberth burnt by Gruffydd ap Rhys in 1116 was probably the ringwork at Sentence, which was destroyed again by the Welsh in 1215. A new castle was built on the existing site on a promontory at Narberth in 1246 by Sir Andrew Perrot and the keep may relate to this period. The castle was captured and destroyed by the Welsh in 1257. It later passed to the Mortimers and the rest of what survives on the site is thought to have been built by them in the 1280s. There was a fire at the castle, probably accidental, in 1299. After Roger Mortimer, Earl of March, was executed for treason in 1330, Narberth was given by Edward III to Henry Gower, Bishop of St Davids. The castle was acquired by Thomas Carew in 1404 and held by him against Owain Glyndwr. Henry VIII granted Narberth to Sir Rhys ap Thomas in 1516. It was neglected after it reverted to the Crown in 1531 and a survey of 1609 describes it as "decayed and wasted for twenty years past and more". The castle is said to have been damaged during a siege in the Civil War but at least part of it seems to have remained inhabited for several years afterwards. Much of the building has disappeared since the ruins were engraved by the Buck brothers in 1740.

The castle had a roughly rectangular enclosure 45m long by 25m wide, or to be more precise, it was a pentagon, since the east side had a slight angle marked by a tower or turret. Nothing remains of the gateway in the NW corner with a tower either over or beside it, and just one high fragment remains of a lofty round keep 12m in diameter above a broad battered base at the NE corner. Old accounts suggest it contained three living rooms over a lofty basement. Rather more survives of the southern half of the castle which comprised a south range and an east range meeting at right angles and towers 10m in diameter on the SW and SE angles. Only one high fragment remains of the SE tower but the SW tower is better preserved. The wall between them has gone but lengths of the west and east curtain walls run northwards from the two towers. Little remains of the hall on the upper level of the south range but the inner wall towards the court of the lower storey survives, with three narrow windows and a doorway. The upper storey of the east range was the great chamber or solar, but all that remains is the vaulted cellar below it, with two windows facing the court and doorways to the west and south. There seems to have been another narrow range on the west side of the court which is said to have contained a gallery on the upper level, probably added by Sir Rhys ap Thomas c1520.

SW Tower at Narberth

Newhouse: interior

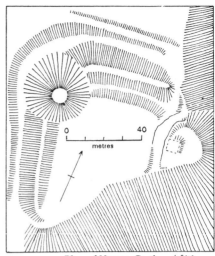

Plan of Nevern Castle 1- 2500

NEVERN   SN 082401

Nevern or Nanhyfer was the original seat of the lordship of Cemmaes and was held by the Normans until 1191, when, despite having sworn an oath to the contrary, the Lord Rhys captured it from William, husband of his own daughter Angharad, and grandson of the builder of the castle, Robert Fitz Martin. In 1194 Rhys was imprisoned in the castle by his own rebellious sons. It was later abandoned in favour of Newport. It lies on the edge of a ravine above the Gamman river and seems to have been developed from an earlier fort, possibly from the Iron Age. It is a triangle with a natural slope defending the long SE side, a single ditch and rampart on the west and a double ditch and rampart system on the north. In the NW corner is a motte with traces of a small tower on the summit, which measures 8m across. The naturally strongest east corner of the bailey is divided off by a rock-cut ditch to form an egg-shaped court 25m long by 20m wide. The court seems to have had a low stone breastwork around a rectangular tower about 9m square, now marked only by a tree-clad mound.

NEWHOUSE   SN 072136

Newhouse, also called Castell Coch, is a ruined 13th century hall-house with a surrounding ditch lying hidden in woods beside a tributary of the Eastern Cleddau. It is 23m long by 10.4m wide over walls up to 1.6m thick. The lowest storey has three loops in the north wall, one loop in each end wall (both later opened out into doorways) and two loops plus a centrally placed doorway with two drawbar slots in the south wall. A narrow service stair lay in the SW corner but the main access to the upper storey was by a doorway just west of that below. Quite how the building was originally divided up inside it uncertain. In the 15th century a thick cross-wall was inserted to close off the eastern end then allowed to decay or only used for storage. The cross-wall has a basement recess and pairs of fireplaces at the level of the second storey and an inserted third storey.

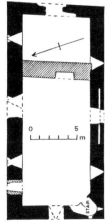

Plan of Newhouse

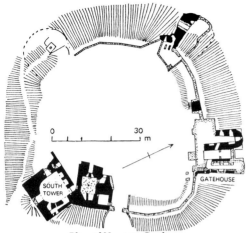

Plan of Newport Castle

Newport Castle

NEWPORT   SN 057388

The castle built here c1200 by William Fitz Martin may have been by the shore at the north end of the long narrow township founded at the same time, where there are remains of an earthwork. The existing site high above the south end of the town was perhaps first occupied when Newport was rebuilt after being destroyed in 1215 by Llywelyn ab Iorwerth. The castle and town were again destroyed by the Welsh in 1257, and the Martins rebuilt the castle in stone c1280-1300. In 1326 the castle passed by marriage to James de Audley. It was forfeited to the Crown on the execution of James, Lord Audley by Henry VII in 1497 but Henry VIII restored Newport to his son in 1534. The castle was sold to William Owen of Henllys in 1543. His son George described the it as "...a strong and lardge castle, moted, garetted, and with towres, and having a lardge courte within". A print of the 1740s shows the building as ruinous with only the gatehouse and NW tower still standing high.

In 1859 the gatehouse on the NE side of a court measuring about 60m across was remodelled as a residence for Sir Thomas Lloyd of Bronwydd and it is still occupied. The entrance was flanked by towers of unequal width but only the larger western tower 6.5m wide still stands. It has rebuilt basal spurs. The polygonal upper stage and and corbelled parapet may be later, perhaps of the 1370s when repairs were ordered, or perhaps after 1408 when a valuation refers to the castle as recently destroyed by Owain Glyndwr. The inner walls flanking the passage are thicker than the outer walls to the east and west and could be relics of a simple rectangular gate tower of c1230-40. A modern loopholed wall (including a tiny fragment of the much more massive original wall) extends from the gatehouse to a NW tower known as the Hunter's Hall. Only the west side now remains, enough to show that it had three storeys over a solid base with tiny basal spurs and that it contained a well. There were latrines where the west curtain adjoined the tower. Little remains of the Kitchen Tower on the west. The small chamber on the site was built after the tower had fallen or been dismantled and is unlikely to be the "Gaole for felons" mentioned by George Owen. Two storeys remain of a D-shaped south tower 12m wide with a square base. The basement is reached directly from the court and has a latrine and three blocked loops. A separate entrance with a carved head above it gives onto a spiral stair to the upper levels and the former south curtain wall-walk. Immediately NE of this tower is a crypt with vaulting spring from a central pier. To the court the room has two narrow loops between two big buttresses. The room above shows no signs of having been a chapel.

Pembroke Castle

PEMBROKE   SM 982016   OP

This superb defensive site was first fortified in 1093, when Dyfed was invaded by Roger de Montgomery after the death of Rhys ap Tewdwr. The castle was handed over to Roger's younger son Arnulf and was the only stronghold in the district which the Welsh failed to capture when they rose against the Normans in 1094. Arnulf was involved in the rebellion of his brother Robert de Bellesme in 1102, and after their defeat Henry I took over Pembroke and entrusted it to a knight named Saer. He was replaced by Gerald de Windsor in 1105. Gilbert de Clare, son of the conqueror of Ceredigion, was created Earl of Pembroke by King Stephen in 1138 and presumably had custody of the castle, although it has no recorded history of that period. Pembroke increased in importance, especially as a port, after Gilbert's son Richard, also nicknamed Strongbow, invaded Ireland in 1169. Henry II presumably stayed at the castle before and after his trip to Ireland to establish his authority there.

In 1189 William Marshal married Richard's heiress Isabel and became Earl of Pembroke. William was one of the greatest men of his day, owing the service of 100 knights for Leinster alone. He began rebuilding the castle in stone. The keep, the walls of the inner ward with an unusual D-shaped gateway, and the Norman hall are all assumed to have been complete by 1207 when the earl, normally high in favour, fell out with King John, who took possession of all his English and Welsh castles. Probably the walls of the outer ward were begun soon after the John restored William to his possessions in 1211. Work upon them would have continued under his eldest son William, who succeeded in 1219 and died in 1231, and was succeeded in turn by his brothers Richard (murdered in Ireland in 1234), Gilbert (killed in a riding accident in 1241), and Walter and Anselm who both died in 1245. None left any children so the vast estates were divided among their five sisters who were all married with families.

Pembroke, Wexford and Goodrich thus passed to the children of the youngest sister, Joan, who died in the 1230s. Her son John de Munchensy died in 1247 during the long and complex division of the Marshal estates, so his share went to his sister Joan, who married William de Valance, the unpopular half-brother of King Henry III. William was never formerly invested with the title of earl although he was sometimes called it and anyway used Pembroke castle as his main seat. He built the splendid new Northern Hall in the inner ward and probably also the St Anne's Bastion. He died in 1296 but his wife Joan lived until 1307, and only then did their son Aylmer succeed to the estate and the title of Earl of Pembroke. After he died in 1324 the earldom and castle passed to Laurence de Hastings, the young grandson of Aymer's eldest sister Isabel. Laurence was the first of three generations of this family who all succeeded as young children. Laurence (who died in 1348) and his son John fought in Edward III's wars against the French. John died in 1375 after three years' captivity in France after being defeated at sea off La Rochelle, and his son John was killed at the age of 17 in a jousting accident in 1389 without being formerly invested in the title and lands.

The Hastings' earls were absentee lords who neglected the castle at Pembroke, which at the time of the scare of a French invasion in 1377 was said to be out of repair and without a garrison or victuals. In June of that year Edward III installed a garrison under Degary Seys, and in July this was doubled in strength to a total of three knights, 67 serjeants-at-arms and 70 archers. After the castle passed to the Crown in 1389 it continued to be neglected, being farmed out to various short-term tenants such as William de Beauchamp who is thought to have plundered lead from the roofs of the domestic buildings. In 1403 Henry V, faced with a crisis caused by Owain Glyndwr's rebellion granted Pembroke, Tenby and Cilgerran to Sir Francis Court. Munitions, including gunpowder for handguns, were sent for the defence of Pembroke in 1405. Pembroke gained another absentee lord in 1413, when Sir Francis died and the castle was given to the King's younger brother Humphrey, created Duke of Gloucester and Earl of Pembroke in 1414. After Duke Humphrey died in 1447, Pembroke was given to William de la Pole, Earl of Suffolk. He was raised to a Dukedom in 1448 but fell from power in 1450, and was killed by pirates after being exiled. Pembroke was then given in dower to Henry VI's consort, Queen Margaret.

In 1454 Jasper Tudor was given the castle and created Earl of Pembroke. In the castle was born his nephew Henry, later Henry VII, posthumous son of Edmund Tudor, Earl of Richmond, the mother being the teenage Lady Margaret Beaufort. Jasper was dispossessed of Pembroke after the Lancastrian defeat at Towton in 1461. William Herbert was instructed to seize the county and in 1462 was formerly created Earl of Pembroke. Jasper managed to briefly regain Pembroke during the Lancastrian restoration of 1470. The second William Herbert, back in possession of Pembroke after the Yorkist revival of 1471, exchanged titles with Edward, Prince of Wales a year before the latter succeeded in 1483 as Edward V. In that year repairs were carried out on the castle and it was garrisoned. The expected invasion by Henry Tudor occurred in 1485 when he landed at Dale. By the end of the year Richard III was dead, Henry was King, and Jasper Tudor restored as Earl of Pembroke until his death in 1495.

The entrance front at Pembroke

Garrison hall at Pembroke

During the 16th century Pembroke was retained by the Crown, although others held the title, Queen Anne Boleyn being Marchioness of Pembroke from 1532 until her execution in 1536, and William Herbert III being created Earl of Pembroke by Edward VI in 1551. It appears that the inner ward was still partly maintained, courts being held within its chambers, whilst the outer ward was leased out for pasture or cultivation.

When the Civil War broke out in 1642 Pembroke was held for Parliament and John Poyer, a former Mayor, took possession of the castle. Their local commander Rowland Laugharne used it as a refuge and the castle remained largely cut off until 1645 although no regular siege was maintained. During this period the vulnerable sections of the outer ward facing the town were doubled in thickness by building against the inside face, the material apparently being obtained by demolishing much of the wall that separated the two wards. In 1648 Poyer and Laugharne became disenchanted with Parliament and held the town and castle against Oliver Cromwell for seven weeks of siege in the summer of that year. The assault was mainly against the narrow eastern section of the town wall, the only part then not protected by a wide stretch of water. After the surrender Poyer was executed and then or soon afterwards the east part of the town wall was demolished and the outer parts of the barbican and the towers along the front of the outer ward of the castle which faced the town were also destroyed, and the battlements knocked off parts of the rest of the building.

In the 1880s the castle enthusiast J.R.Cobb carried out some repairs and excavated the remains of the inner gate. In 1928 the castle was acquired by Major General Sir Ivor Philipps, by whom the vegetation covering the ruins was removed, and then the parts destroyed in the mid 17th century slighting were restored. The General's daughter in 1959 conveyed the castle to a Trust which still administers it.

Pembroke is the largest and best preserved castle of the period 1190-1245 in Wales. Among medieval castles in the whole of Britain it has few peers in terms of its naturally scenic and defensive position and degree of preservation. The castle lies on a flat topped platform at the end of a ridge occupied by the town. On either side of the ridge were tidal creeks which joined beyond the castle and then connected with the larger estuary of Milford Haven. The north creek has long ceased to be tidal as a result of a dam associated with a mill and the southern creek has been drained. The area enclosed by the castle walls is roughly egg-shaped and measures 150m from the point of the promontory (there rising 12m above the creeks) at the NW to the outer gate at the SE, by 100m wide. About a quarter of the total enclosed space is closed off at the NW end as an inner ward containing the celebrated keep and all the main domestic buildings. This inner ward presumably corresponds to the original ringwork of the 1090s which, as far as is known, only had timber defences until the 1190s.

The inner ward is so well defended by nature that on its north and west sides the defending wall, although quite thick, has its walkway less than a metre above the court. There is a tiny turret on the NW corner and close to it is the massive base of what is thought to have been a single storey building upon which was mounted a catapult commanding the Mill Pond. The much higher curtain wall on the vulnerable SE side had a ditch in front (now filled in) and was flanked by a rectangular turret at the east end, the round Dungeon Tower further south, and the so called Horseshoe Gate. The latter (destroyed to within a metre of the ground along with the curtain as far as the Dungeon Tower to provide material for reinforcing the outer wall in the 1640s) was a D-shaped structure projecting 11m beyond the wall and being over 9m wide. A gate on the west side gave onto what was probably a small open court with the wall embattled on both sides so as to command both it and the field. Another gateway then led through the inner wall itself. The SW corner of the inner ward is filled by a room nearly 14m long covered with a high pointed vault and known as the Western Hall. It has a fireplace, several loops, one of which covered the outer entrance of the Horseshoe Gate, and a latrine is provided in a turret at the west end. Probably this was a garrison mess-hall. The larger building against its north face, the east and north walls of which are reduced to the ground, may have been a stable-block.

The Northern Hall at Pembroke

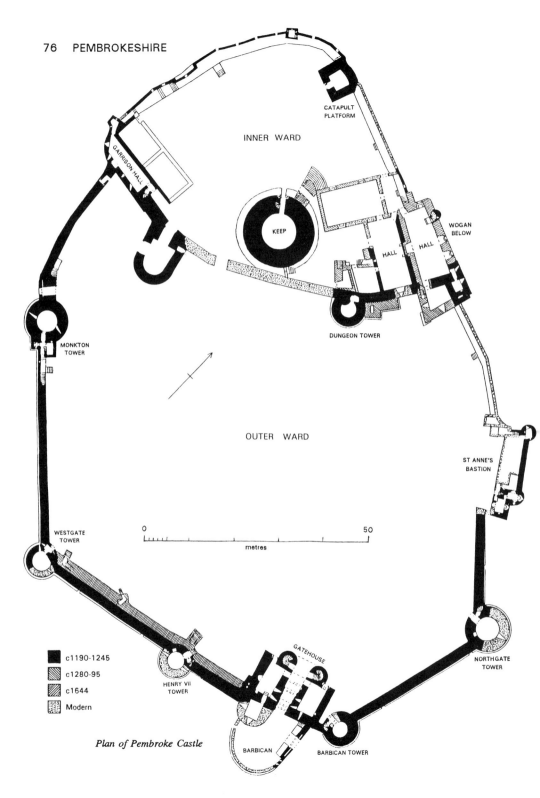

INNER WARD

CATAPULT
PLATFORM

GARRISON HALL

KEEP

WOGAN
BELOW

HALL HALL

MONKTON
TOWER

DUNGEON TOWER

OUTER WARD

ST ANNE'S
BASTION

WESTGATE
TOWER

0   50
|‖‖‖‖‖|_____|_____|_____|_____|_____|
              metres

■ c1190-1245

▨ c1280-95

▧ c1644

▦ Modern

GATEHOUSE

HENRY VII
TOWER

NORTHGATE
TOWER

BARBICAN

BARBICAN TOWER

Plan of Pembroke Castle

In the east corner of the inner ward are two hall blocks side by side. Neither can have been well lighted since the keep would have put them in shadow and the further one faces north. The southern and plainer of the two is the original hall of the 1190s. Raised over a storage basement, it has an original fireplace on the south side. The triple lancet east window is a modern restoration. Connecting the old hall to the Dungeon Tower is a square mid 13th century block containing on the upper storey the withdrawing room. This apartment has an original fireplace on the south, a west facing oriel window of c1490, and a door on the east to a latrine block added against the curtain beside the Dungeon tower. The splendid northern hall block dates from the late 13th century. It is embattled with the corners raised up as turrets and is connected by a spiral stair in a round turret on the north side to the large natural cavern known as the Wogan, the floor of which is about 4m above the waters of the creek. A wall of the 1190s closed the cavern mouth except for a watergate (now secured by a grille), over which is a window with twin lancets. Both the hall itself and the kitchen below it have window embrasures with seats in the north and west walls, fireplaces in the middle of the SW wall (backing onto the older hall), and entrances at the NW end. The SE end of the block (projecting beyond the original curtain of the inner ward and enveloping the older latrine turret) contained a private chamber with window embrasures with seats facing SW and SE over a buttery. Extending towards the keep from the west end of the older hall is a much restored late 13th century building containing a room 13m long by 7.5m wide with windows in the side walls. This room must be that in which the business of the court of the county of Pembroke was conducted.

The keep at Pembroke

Northern Hall at Pembroke

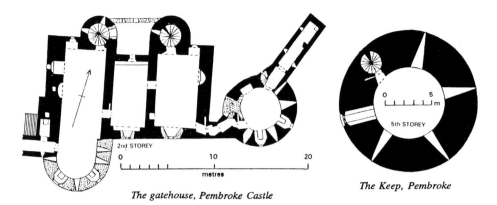

The gatehouse, Pembroke Castle

The Keep, Pembroke

The keep lies immediately behind the base of the inner ward SE wall. It is 15.7m in diameter over walling 4m thick above the broad spreading base and rises 22m high. There are five storeys below a dome vault upon the crown of which was a small central turret. Surrounding it were two levels of parapets, although it appears that main purpose of the upper parapet was to provide a inner wall for when timber hoarding enveloping the bottom parapet was erected in times of war. The only original entrance (except for a postern connected by a timber bridge to the inner ward SE wall) is that reached by a wide stair rising beside the end gable of the court room. The dressings have gone but the deep draw-bar hole remains. From here a spiral stair rises to the upper levels and descends to an unlit basement later provided with its own entrance from the court). There are no latrines in the keep but the second and third storeys have fireplaces on the west side. The arrow-slits of the middle three storeys all have narrow embrasures and admitted little light. The third and fourth storeys each have a single window of two lancets under a pointed outer head, but again the embrasures (with seats) are narrow and only admitted a modest amount of light. It is difficult to accept this uncomfortably-appointed keep as anything other than a refuge.

Except for the parts thickened in the 1640s, the walls of the outer court are mostly 2m thick and 10m to 12m high. The wall between the Westgate and Monkton towers has an exceptionally high parapet so the present wall-walk must have been intended to be enclosed as a vaulted gallery with another walkway on top. Projecting from the north side is the St Ann's Bastion, a curious affair with two round turrets facing north and a rectangular turret on the east, between which and the adjacent curtain is the Millport postern. On the east and west sides of the court are the Northgate and Monkton towers, both around 10m in diameter. The outer parts of the former were rebuilt in the 1930s and have authentic looking twin-light windows of primitive design on the second and third storeys. The little-restored Monkton Tower has just two storeys between which there is no direct access. Latrines are contained in a square turret on the SE side, and there is a stair turret on the NW rising above a postern called Monkton Port opening onto the natural rock face. The towers along the vulnerable 70m long face of the south side of the outer ward are smaller (7m - 7.5m in diameter) and perhaps represent an earlier phase of construction. The Westgate, Henry VII (supposedly his birthplace) and Barbican towers are full rounds whilst the Bygate tower is a D-shaped structure forming part of the gatehouse. All were blown up c1648-9 and have had their outer parts rebuilt in the 1930s except for the Barbican Tower, where the inner part was damaged instead. This tower is effectively an adjunct of the gatehouse and the two structures are joined by passages at the upper levels.

In front of the gatehouse is a D-shaped barbican with its rebuilt outer gate facing east. The main gateway passage was closed by two portcullises and lies between rectangular guard rooms commanding it with arrow-loops. The second and third storeys of the gatehouse repeat the layout, with larger rooms with fireplaces set on either side of unheated central rooms. The western rooms are nearly 14m long as they extend into the D-shaped Bygate Tower. Flanking the passageway on the inner side of the gatehouse are two round staircase turrets. A flying arch was later built to connect these, and two small upper rooms were provided above it.

The walls around the town still mostly remain in the form of a thin and much patched revetment now lacking a parapet. There were gates on each side near the castle but the main approach was to the much more accessible (and vulnerable) East Gate, now destroyed. There are remains of three similar round towers about 7m in diameter spaced about 19m apart at the east end of the south side. One is just a fragment, another now bears a gazebo, whilst the third remains in a more complete state with a dome vault over its upper storey and narrow slits flanking the main wall. These towers were entered by means of steps from the interior up onto their roofs, and then spiral stairs led down. A fourth tower on the south, much further west, has gone. Projecting boldly from the NE corner so as to flank the curved face of the eastern walls is Barnard's Tower, a fine structure 8.8m in diameter, containing two living rooms over an unlit basement, with a dome-vault on top. It is entered through a forebuilding with a latrine and portcullis groove at the level of the lower room, which has a fireplace. The tower must have been inhabited by an important official of some kind. Not far west is a solid round tower 6m in diameter.

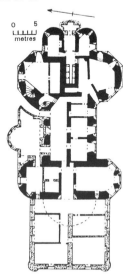

Plan of Picton Castle

Picton Castle

PICTON   SN 016135 & 011134   G

The original castle of Picton lay on the motte to the east of the present building. By the late 13th century the estate had reverted to the barony of Wiston, then held by the Wogans. A new stone castle was built by Sir John Wogan, a man of some importance who held the office of Justiciar of Ireland from 1295 until 1308. It had an unusual plan, having a large low-walled court containing within it at the west end a two storey block about 25m long by 12m wide with three storey D-shaped towers up to 10m in diameter projecting from each end of the north and south sides, plus another tower at the west end, and a projecting gatehouse with round corner towers about 5m in diameter at the east end. The main block contained a hall over an undercroft into which the original entrance admitted, and the five D-shaped towers each contained two upper living rooms over a basement. A Buck print of 1740 shows the SE tower as having trefoil-headed lancet windows on the top storey and corbelled parapets with arrow loops in the merlons on the towers.

The castle is thought to have been occupied by Owain Glyndwr's forces in 1405. About that time it passed by marriage to Owen Dwnn of Carmarthen who inserted large new traceried windows in the hall and also altered the gateway. In the 1480s another heiress brought Picton to Sir Thomas Philipps of Cilsant, whose descendants still own it. Sir John Philipps purchased a baronetcy from James I for £1,095, and in the 17th and 18th centuries the family was the most important in Pembrokeshire. The castle was stormed by a Royalist force in 1645. In the 1690s the castle was altered by Sir John Philipps. An extra storey was added over the hall, some of the tower rooms were given new sash windows, a terrace being created at the south end to give access to a new upper entrance, and most of the outer wall demolished. Sir John, 6th baronet remodelled the interior in 1749-52. The hall now has a gallery upon which is a rare Snetzler organ. Sir Richard, 7th baronet, created Lord Milford in 1776, demolished the tower at the west end c1800 and replaced it by a large castellated block of four storeys. The existing Norman style entrance was added in place of an 18th century porch by Richard Grant Philipps in the 1840s. The present owner has had a 19th century attic storey on the main block removed and this part re-roofed.

Picton Castle

Plans of Roch Castle

Roch Castle

ROCH   SM 881212   V

Roch takes its name from the volcanic outcrop upon which the tower is perched. It was built by the de la Roche family of which Adam in the late 12th century is the first recorded, and Thomas, d1420, was the last. The tower may have been built in the 1260s by John de la Roche, who married a niece of Thomas Wallensis, Bishop of St Davids. From an entrance somewhat above ground level on the west side there was access into the main hall and down to a cellar partly filled by the natural rock. Beyond the hall is another chamber with access to a vaulted oratory in a square turret projecting NE from the round end of the U-shaped building. Originally there was just one more storey above but at a later date the corbelled parapet was heightened to accommodate a fourth storey with a new parapet above it. It appears that it was intended that a court should accompany the tower but it uncertain whether it was actually ever built. From 1420 until it was purchased in 1601 by William Walter of Trefran, the castle was jointly held by the Ferrers and Langueville families. During the 16th century the tower was remodelled and given many mullioned windows. The Earl of Carberry garrisoned the castle for King Charles in 1642. It surrendered to Colonel Rowland Laugharne in February 1644 but was recaptured (along with many animals for feeding the Parliamentarian troops) by Sir Charles Gerard in July the same year, and held by the Royalists until early 1645. John Harries of Trefacwm purchased the castle in the late 18th century but soon sold it to a neighbour, Rees Stokes of Cuffern. By then it was a ruin. John Wynford Phillips, later Viscount St Davids, bought the castle in 1899. The 3rd Viscount sold the restored castle to Lord Kenswood in 1954 and in 1965 it was sold again. It is now hired out as a visitors' holiday home.

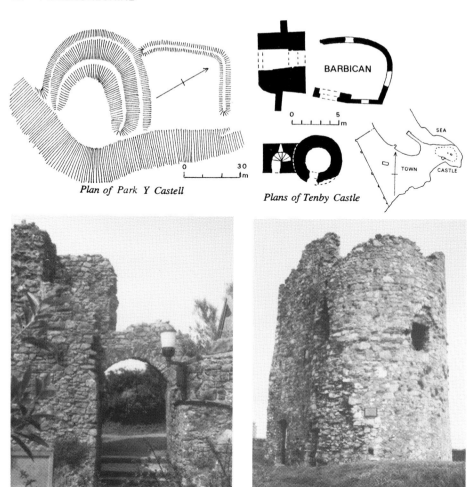

Plan of Park Y Castell

BARBICAN

Plans of Tenby Castle

Gateway at Tenby

Tenby Castle

Outer wall at Tenby

ST DAVIDS   SM 744252

High above the west side of the valley of the Alun 0.7km WSW of the Cathedral is a
the site of a castle now called Parc-Y-Castell assumed to have been erected by one
of the 12th century Bishops of St Davids. It comprises a ringwork measuring 30m by
40m with a high rampart and deep ditch except on the naturally well defended SE
side. To the north are traces of a slight rampart enclosing a bailey 40m square.

TENBY   SN 138005   F

Surprisingly little is known about this strongly sited castle on a rocky peninsular about
30m high protected by the walls of the town on the landward side. The remains lying
on what is now a public garden comprise a modest gateway with short sections of
breastwork on either side, a later D-shaped barbican in front of the gateway, a length
of low embattled wall on the other side of the rock, a round tower on the highest point
of the site, and some walls embedded in what is now the museum. None of these can
be closely dated or form any recognisable usual sort of castle plan. The round tower
is too small to be regarded as a keep, being just 5.3m in diameter, and lacking features
of interest. It could, however, have served as a lighthouse or beacon stance. A square
stair turret 3m wide has been added against its west side.

There was a castle at Tenby by 1153 when it was captured by Maredudd and Rhys
ap Gruffydd in revenge for the severe wounding of their brother Cadell by members
of the garrison. The attackers broke down the gate at night after marching across the
sands from Amroth and they slew the garrison. Maelgwn ap Rhys destroyed the town
and castle in 1187, and in 1260 the town, and perhaps the castle, were taken by
Llywelyn ap Gruffydd. The town walls are of late 13th century date but were
heightened and improved in the 1450s by Jasper Tudor, Earl of Pembroke. They
remain almost intact although three of the four gates were destroyed between 1781
and 1811. With the town securely walled the castle became little more than a store
and barracks and was usually in a neglected condition. It belonged to the earldom of
Pembroke and in 1378 Richard II entrusted Sir William Beauchamp to hold the castle
during the minority of John Hastings. A survey of 1386 reveals it in a sorry state with
decayed gates, falling curtain walls, and severe decay to the chamber over the main
gate and the "lordyschamber" because their lead roofs had been removed.

It is uncertain whether the castle was still regarded as defensible in its own right
in 1642 when Mayor David Hammond repaired the town walls and held Tenby for
Parliament. Thomas Wyatt, one of the inhabitants, betrayed Tenby to the Earl of
Carberry in August 1643. A seaborne attack by Richard Swanley was beaten off but
the town was stormed by Laugharne in 1644, although Wyatt escaped to Bristol. The
Parliamentary garrison later defected to the Royalist cause while the Governor, Colonel
Rice Powell, was away, but in May 1648 Cromwell breached the town wall with
cannon, and the town was promptly surrendered, 20 cannon being captured.

Little remains of the seaward defences of the town but the two lengths of landward
facing wall remain almost complete. The wall averaged about 1.4m thick and has a
wall-walk 4m above ground. The high parapet has two levels of loops, the uppermost
presumably served by a wooden upper walkway. There is a drum tower on the NW
corner, and a D-shaped tower with its basement pierced for pedestrians to pass
through lies to the south. Further on is the only surviving gateway out of four.
Protecting it is a U-shaped barbican like the Horseshoe Gate at Pembroke. It is now
known as the Five Arches because embrasures which once served arrow-loops have
been broken out for vehicles to pass through. Only the round arch facing north was
a gateway. Beyond it lies a 15th century square tower with keyhole shaped gunloops.

Upton Castle

Upton: Plan

UPTON   SN 021047   G

The remains of this 13th century castle on a ridge above the Carew River comprise a north facing gateway with a narrow arch with a portcullis groove set between two of a row of three round towers about 4.5m in diameter with parapets on corbelling. Between the gateway and the NE tower lies a two storey block 4m wide by 8m long internally. The main apartments probably lay on the west side of a small nearly square court where there is a much altered and extended block of uncertain date. The castle was built by the Malephants, the earliest of which on record is Walter, who married Avice de la Roche and was killed fighting the Welsh near Cilgerran in 1258. Effigies of several Malephants lie in the adjacent chapel to the east. Stephen, last of the line, died in the 1490s leaving a daughter Alice who married Owen ap Gruffydd. Their descendant Rhys anglicised his surname to Bowen in 1564. In the late 18th century Upton was sold by co-heiresses to John Tasker. In the 20th century it has been a residence of the Neale family. The grounds and chapel are open to the public.

Upton Castle

WISTON   SN 022181   V

Wiston takes its name from Wizo, a Fleming to whom Henry I granted the lordship of Daugleddau, a tract of land between the East and West Cleddau rivers, and who died c1130. The castle was sited to protect the northern flank of this estate. It has a mound about 12m high bearing the remains of a late 12th century shell keep with a wall 1.6m thick (above the plinth) enclosing a court up to 12m across. The wall survives to a height of 2.5m on the south side where it is pierced by a round arched gateway but has fallen down the slope on the north. The oval bailey on flat ground to the south measures 125m by 80m and has a bank 1m high and a ditch, but never had stone walls. In 1146 the castle was attacked by Cadell, Maredudd, and Rhys, the sons of Gruffydd ap Rhys ap Tewdwr, but their forces were "too weak to master it" until Hywel ab Owain devised "certain battering engines" to aid them. In 1188 the castle was visited by Archbishop Baldwin and Gerald de Barri, and in the following year it withstood a siege by Maelgwyn ap Rhys. Hywel Sais made a surprise attack on the castle in 1193 and managed to take prisoner the lord and his family. The Flemings recaptured the castle on Whit Sunday 1195. Henry III exhorted all the local landowners to aid the rebuilding of the castles of Wiston and Narberth by William, Earl Marshal, after Llywelyn ab Iorwerth captured and destroyed them in 1220, the neighbourhood being ravaged. Recent clearance has shown that the shell wall was then thickened by 0.6m on the inside and provided with crosswalls for internal buildings. The Earl was then guardian of an infant Wizo heiress who later married Sir Walter de Herford. Wiston later passed to heiresses, one of whom married one of the Wogans. They later obtained the whole barony and held it until 1779, but transferred the seat to Picton.

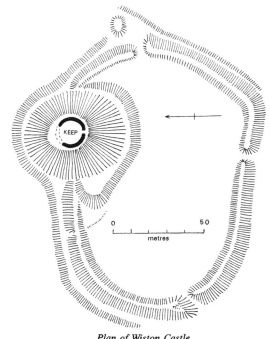

Plan of Wiston Castle

Shell Keep at Wiston

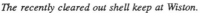

The recently cleared out shell keep at Wiston.

Town wall at Tenby

OTHER CASTLES IN PEMBROKESHIRE

BEGELLY SN 117072 Last traces of mound with bailey to NW now removed.

BLACKBRIDGE SM 919064 Motte by junction of streams 1km ENE of Milford Haven.

CALDY SS 140963 At the NE corner of the priory cloister is a 14th century tower with a corbelled and embattled parapet containing over a vaulted cellar a room for the prior with a latrine in a NE turret.

CAMROSE SM 927198 Motte 7.5m high with traces of bailey.

CASTELL CRYCHYDD SN 261348 Mound rising 5m to hollow summit 9m across with traces of stonework. Bailey platform 27m long by just 9m wide.

CASTELL CYNEN SN 155146 Very overgrown ringwork 36m across and 3.5m high.

CASTELL FARTIN SM 943368 Mound in woods by stream 1km south of Goodwick.

CASTELL LLAINFAWR SN 151374 Partial ringwork 2m high beside swampy hollow.

CASTELL PENGAWSAI SN 110280 A small motte.

CASTELL POETH SM 897377 Damaged motte by cross-roads north of St Nicholas.

CASTELL Y DRIM SN 064196 Small mound by farm above railway.

CASTELL Y FRAN SN 081222 Mound rising 4.5m to top 7m across with good view.

CASTLEBYTHE SN 021290 Motte rising up to 6m to a summit 12m across. Oval bailey 70m long by 50m wide with bank 3.5m high now gone.

CASTLE MARTIN SR 915984 Remains of weak ringwork and bailey.

CASTLE MORRIS SM 903316 Nothing now remains of the motte here.

DINGSTOPPLE SN 061186 Small mound with wet ditch by stream.

DRIM SN 014196 Damaged ringwork.

DYFFRYN MAWR SN 175351 Ditched motte rising 6m to top 18m across with central depression and traces of stonework. Positioned between two streams.

EAST BLOCKHOUSE SM 841029 Remains of block added later to vanished round gun battery of c1540 guarding the entrance to Milford Haven on cliff above Rat Island. A 19th century fort replaced the similar West Blockhouse on opposite shore.

EGLWYSWRW SN 139383 Partial ringwork rising to 2.5m high at SW corner of small enclosure 27m by 18m.

GREAT RUDBAXTON SM 961205 Mound by the church.

GREEN CASTLE SN 128142 Mound rising 4.5m to top 9m across. Bailey to NW.

HAYCASTLE SM 897256 6m high mound by farm 1km SE of church.

HENRY'S MOAT SN 044 275 Mound rising 4.5m high to summit 10m across. Ditch only survives on the west side.

LETTERSTON SM 938295 Named after its Flemish builder, Letard Littleking, killed in 1137. A damaged motte remains to the south of the village street.

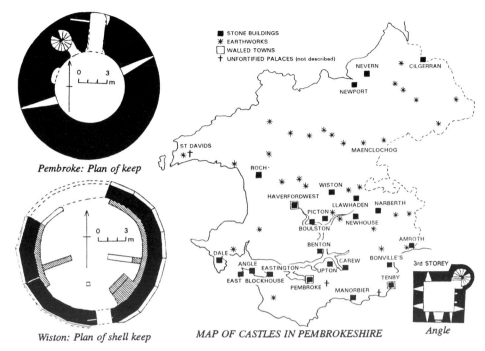

Pembroke: Plan of keep

Wiston: Plan of shell keep

MAP OF CASTLES IN PEMBROKESHIRE

Angle

LITTLE NEWCASTLE SM 980289 Motte and bailey remains removed 1965.
LLANFYRNACH SN 219312 Motte and bailey to NW of the church.
LLANGLYDWEN SN 177268 Mound on spur above Afon Taf.
MAENOROWEN SM 943368 Small ringwork on the end of a ridge.
MANIAN FAWR SN 150479 Motte by farm track above deep gully.
MINWEAR SN 062135 Mound in woods above Pen Glyn.
NANT PERCHELLAN SN 172434 Heavily overgrown mound above Afon Pillau.
NEW MOAT SN 063253 Ditched motte with counterscarp bank and weak bailey.
PANT Y CADNO SN 112226 Mound high above Eastern Cleddau and a tributary.
PARC Y MARL SN 047245 Mound near farm.
PEN YR ALLT SN 158420 Ringwork with rampart discontinued on strong SE side.
POINTZ SM 830237 Named after Ponce, a tenant of Bishop Peter de Leia in the
    1180s. Mound by Pointz Castle Farm rising 5.5m to top 10m across.
PUNCHESTON SN 009298 Ringwork with rampart on sides away from Afon Anghof.
RUDBAXTON RATH SM 985188 Ringwork and bailey inside much older fort.
SENTENCE SN 110116 Just a section of the ditch now remains beside a path.
ST ISHMAELS SM 835076 Mound north of village.
STACKPOLE SR 977961 The cellars of Stackpole Court may be part of former tower
    house or hall-house.
WALWYN'S SM 873030 Ringwork with bailey & possibly stonework. Seat of barony.
WOLFSCASTLE SM 958265 Motte on landward side of bailey on promontory above
    Western Cleddau. Mentioned in 1229 and possibly in 1326.

The episcopal palaces at Lamphrey and St Davids have been left out of this book, as
although they were embattled no part of them could be defended. The same is true
of the thinly walled hall-house at Lydstep, also owned by the bishops, and of the
manor house of the Perrot family at Haroldston, and also Priory Farm at Monkton.

GLOSSARY OF TERMS

Ashlar	- Masonry of blocks with even faces and square edges.
Aumbry	- A recess or cupboard for storage.
Bailey	- A defensible space enclosed by a wall or palisade and a ditch.
Barbican	- A building or enclosure defending a castle entrance.
Bastion	- A squat projecting tower rising no higher than the curtain wall.
Batter	- An inward inclination of a wall face.
Caput	- The principal seat or administrative centre of an estate.
Corbel	- A projecting bracket supporting other stonework or timbers.
Curtain Wall	- A high enclosing stone wall around a bailey.
Embattled	- Provided with a parapet with indentations (crenellations).
Hall House	- A building containing a hall on the uppermost of two storeys.
Jamb	- The side of a doorway, window, or other opening.
Keep	- A citadel or ultimate strongpoint. Originally called a donjon.
Light	- A compartment of a window.
Loop	- A small opening to admit light or for the discharge of missiles.
Machicolation	- A slot for dropping stones or shooting missiles at assailants.
Merlons	- The upstanding portions of a crenellated parapet.
Moat	- A ditch, water filled or dry, around an enclosure.
Motte	- A steeply sided flat topped mound, usually mostly man-made.
Oriel	- A bay window projecting out from a wall above ground level.
Quoin	- A dressed or shaped stone at the corner of a building.
Parapet	- A wall for protection at any sudden drop.
Plinth	- The projecting base of a wall. It may be battered or stepped.
Portcullis	- A wooden gate designed to rise and fall in vertical grooves.
Postern	- A secondary gateway or doorway. A back entrance.
Quoin	- Dressed (i.e. carefully shaped) stone at a corner of a building.
Ravelin	- Triangular enclosure protecting the approach to an entrance.
Ringwork	- An embanked enclosure of more modest size than a bailey.
Shell Keep	- A small stone walled enclosure on top of a motte.
Solar	- The lord's private living room, usually doubling as a bed-chamber.
Tower House	- Self contained house with the main rooms stacked vertically.
Wall-walk	- A walkway on top of a wall, protected by a parapet.
Ward	- A stone walled defensive enclosure.

FURTHER READING

Archeologia Cambrensis.
Castellarium Anglicanum, D J C King, two vols, 1983.
Castles of Dyfed, Paul R Davis, 1987.
Castles of Pembrokeshire, Dilwyn Miles, various editions.
Castles and Strongholds of Pembrokshire, Thomas Stickings, 1973.
Castles of The Welsh Princes, Paul R Davis, 1988.
Journals of the antiquarian societies of Cardigan (Ceredigion) & Carmarthen.
Newport Castle, David M Browne & David Percival, R.C.A.H.M, 1988.
Norman Castles in Britain, Derek Renn, 1968.
Royal Commission on Ancient and Historical monuments inventory: Carmarthenshire.
Royal Commission on Ancient and Historical monuments inventory: Pembrokeshire.
The Medieval Towns of Wales, Ian Soulsby, 1983.
Cadw pamphlets: Carreg Cennan, Cilgerran, Kidwelly, Llansteffan, Llawhaden.
Other pamphlets: Aberystwyth, Carew, Manorbier, Pembroke and Picton.